Well-being in Danish Cities

Please cite this publication as:
OECD (2016), *Well-being in Danish Cities*, OECD Publishing, Paris.
http://dx.doi.org/10.1787/9789264265240-en

ISBN 978-92-64-26523-3 (print)
ISBN 978-92-64-26524-0 (PDF)

Photo credits: Cover © cienpiesnf - Fotolia.com.

Corrigenda to OECD publications may be found on line at: *www.oecd.org/about/publishing/corrigenda.htm*.

Foreword

Individuals' material conditions and quality of life and the cohesiveness of communities in the present and in the future are in part shaped by the circumstances experienced in the place where people live. Well-being indicators are an important tool for government at different scales to identify the needs of citizens and the policy domains where the demand for progress is the greatest. They are also instruments to raise awareness among citizens on the living conditions in their communities, foster their participation in the public debate and, ultimately, build trust in government.

With the How's Life in Your Region project, a part of the Better Life Initiative, the OECD launched in 2014 an innovative approach to measuring well-being at regional and local levels and understanding what needs to be done to achieve greater progress for all. This report extends the measurement of well-being to more detailed territorial levels of analysis, namely that of cities, which reflect the spaces where individuals set out their daily lives.

Denmark is the first country to have applied the OECD Regional Well-Being Framework to the scale of the city, by providing evidence based on objective and subjective indicators for 11 dimensions in the 5 major Danish cities. In this report, cities are identified to reflect the place where people live and work, with an approach that overcomes administrative boundaries to account for the economic functions of cities in Denmark. With such an approach, this report provides evidence on well-being trends and drivers, income inequality within and across cities, spatial segregation, and specific snapshots for each city.

The report also offers a useful basis for better understanding local assets and constraints for urban and regional development in Denmark. Beyond the benefits for Denmark, this report can provide an example for other countries wanting to pursue a similar comprehensive approach to understanding the drivers of well-being of their citizens at the scale where it matters the most.

Acknowledgements

This report is part of the work on How's Life in Your Region? project produced by the OECD Public Governance and Territorial Development Directorate under the leadership of Rolf Alter and its Regional Development Policy Division led by Joaquim Oliveira Martins. The report was made possible through the support of the Region of Southern Denmark.

The OECD Secretariat is grateful to the co-ordinating team at the Statistical Unit of the Region of Southern Denmark, led by Rune Stig Mortensen, Kresten N. Laursen, Johanna Lundström and Katrine Prytz Larsen. The Secretariat would also like to acknowledge the representatives of the Danish municipalities, the Region of Southern Denmark and the Central Denmark Region for sharing their perspectives during the OECD field mission on 14 and 15 September 2016.

This report was co-ordinated by Paolo Veneri and drafted by Paolo Veneri and Justine Boulant under the supervision of Monica Brezzi from the Regional Development Policy Division of the OECD's Directorate of Public Governance and Territorial Development. Johanna Lundström and Kresten N. Laursen (Region of Southern Denmark) contributed to Chapter 2. Daniel Sánchez-Serra helped with the data in Chapter 1. The manuscript has benefited from comments from OECD colleagues and national delegates to the OECD Working Party on Territorial Indicators.

Jennifer Allain and Pilar Philip are kindly acknowledged for preparing the manuscript for publication.

Table of contents

Tables

Figures

Boxes

Executive summary

Danish people have high living standards in many dimensions of life. They enjoy among the highest levels of safety, civic engagement and social network support in the OECD, and the highest levels of life satisfaction. Compared to other OECD countries, people living in Denmark today have higher educational attainments and longer lives. They also participate more in elections and are less likely to be victims of violent crimes. On the other hand, the long-term unemployment rate and housing expenditures have increased in Denmark. There are relatively small differences in people's well-being across Danish regions, but much less is known at the smaller scale, such as that of cities and their neighbourhoods, which matter most for people's day-to-day lives.

This report provides an assessment of people's well-being in the five major Danish cities: Copenhagen, Aarhus, Aalborg, Esbjerg and Odense, and compares living standards there to those in the rest of the country. These cities account for 58% of the national population and 61% of total employment, although they cover only 19% of the national territory. Cities in Denmark have grown faster in terms of population and employment than the rest of the country since 2000, with the strongest growth in the largest cities, such as Copenhagen and Aarhus. People living in the major cities are also much younger, on average, than the rest of the country and this gap has been increasing over the last decade. At the beginning of 2016, the share of people over 65 years old was 17% on average in Danish cities, while it was 42% in the rest of Denmark.

An accurate measurement of people's well-being at the scale of people's daily lives is important for designing and implementing more effective policies and to help cities flourish. To assess well-being, this report considers Danish cities from a perspective of "functional boundaries" (also called "city-regions" or "functional urban areas" [FUAs]). Such spaces are where people move daily for their activities and they include several municipalities. According to this definition, cities are composed of a central and dense area, known as the "city core", and a surrounding area with lower population density but a strong connection to the core, referred to as the "commuting zone".

As part of the OECD Better Life Initiative, the OECD work on measuring regional well-being monitors well-being outcomes and their trends in the 395 regions of OECD countries. Building on this initiative, this report represents the first assessment of well-being outcomes by the OECD at the scale of the city, with an approach that overcomes administrative boundaries to account for the full array of economic functions of cities in Denmark. At the scale of cities, the use of well-being indicators can help identify citizens' needs and priorities, and mobilise citizens and relevant stakeholders in interconnected areas that often lack a formal governance system.

Main findings

Households in Copenhagen have, on average, 15% higher income than those in the rest of Denmark, a lower gap than that observed on average in the OECD (18%) between metropolitan areas (FUAs with at least 500 000 inhabitants) and other locations.

Since 2000, disposable household income has been growing in all Danish cities, the most quickly in Copenhagen and Aarhus. Aarhus also shows a faster increase in tertiary educational attainment by its working-age inhabitants. However, income inequality has been rising as well, mostly driven by faster growth in the top 20% of the income distribution.

While household income has fully recovered from the economic crisis, labour participation rates have been stagnating or declining since 2008, with the city of Odense showing the fastest decline. Unemployment is concentrated in the cores of Danish cities, with the highest gap between the core and the commuting zone observed in Esbjerg and Aarhus. Life expectancy is, on average, higher in cities than in the rest Denmark, particularly those with a larger population and higher median income. However, large differences are observed within cities. In the case of Copenhagen, for example, there is a difference of almost 4.5 years in life expectancy depending on the municipality of residence. The municipalities with the highest and second-lowest life expectancies in Denmark are both located in the FUA of Copenhagen.

Unlike in most OECD countries, population growth has been stronger in the city cores of Danish cities than in their commuting zones since 2006. However, living conditions in the core are not always the same as those in the periphery. For example, exposure to violent crime is higher in the cores than in the commuting zones, despite the generally high safety levels in all cities. This difference is particularly large in Copenhagen, where crime levels in the core are double those in the commuting zone. Similarly, households in the city core have, on average, lower income than households in the commuting zone, with gaps ranging from -15% in Copenhagen and Esbjerg to -11% in Odense.

Within cities, people tend to live close to others who are similar to them. For example, concentrations of unemployed people in specific areas are relatively higher in the cores of Danish cities, with the exception of Copenhagen. Rich and poor urban residents often live in clearly separate neighbourhoods, which can produce socio-economic segregation. In the case of Danish cities, spatial segregation by income is stronger among the poorest households, a pattern similar to that found in Dutch cities. It is the opposite of what has been observed in Canada, France and the United States, where the most affluent groups are those showing the highest tendency to concentrate in specific neighbourhoods. People living in disadvantaged areas often have lower quality public services, and this might undermine their opportunities for the future.

A better understanding of how urban development affects people's well-being can help policy makers design and monitor development strategies and prioritise and target policy interventions to ensure they address the most pressing needs.

Chapter 1.

Well-being in cities: Rationale and definitions

This chapter provides the framework to assess people's well-being in Danish cities. It defines the boundaries of the five cities – also called "city-regions" or "functional urban areas" – that are analysed in the report, based on the OECD methodology, which is consistently applied across countries. The chapter describes the five cities and provides basic socio-demographic statistics, both in levels and trends, over the last decade. Finally, the chapter presents the OECD framework to measure well-being at subnational level, highlighting specific issues and challenges that should be taken into account when working at the scale of cities.

Introduction

The ultimate objective of policy is to improve people's well-being. A solid evidence base is increasingly important to ensure the effectiveness of policy, both in its design and evaluation. Given the importance of subnational governments in affecting people's life, usable evidence and data are increasingly needed to support policy design, raise awareness among citizens and monitor the progress of society. In this context, the OECD has worked extensively to provide a framework and data to assess well-being outcomes at the national and regional levels, according to 11 dimensions (material conditions and quality of life) (OECD, 2011; 2014a).

Danish people have high living standards in many dimensions of life and show relatively low regional disparities. However, much less knowledge is available on what happens at smaller geographies. Measuring well-being in cities is, in fact, challenging as data are not always easily available at such a scale, despite the fact that cities are crucial geographies for the daily life of people. As in practically all developed countries, most of the population in Denmark can be considered "urban". However, drawing a net line between urban and rural areas – or just between urban and non-urban – is not straightforward and, above all, can be misleading. It is largely documented that the majority of the population – almost 60% in the case of Denmark – nowadays lives in agglomerations that include large and densely inhabited settlements and low-density or even rural areas that are relatively close and functionally linked to one another. These agglomerations are often called "city-regions" or "functional urban areas" and they are based on the daily movements of the people who live, work and consume within a certain space, rather than on a legal or administrative boundary of a municipality.

City-regions have gained a lot of attention both in the scientific and political debate, since they represent – in a relatively small portion of territory – the major concentration of population and economic activities of a country and they largely contribute to the national performance and social progress. During the last 15 years, for example, the population in the 5 main city-regions of Denmark (Copenhagen, Aarhus, Aalborg, Odense and Esbjerg) has grown significantly more than the rest of the country (10% and 2.5%, respectively).

The first concern about city-regions regards the identification of their boundaries and the assessment of their economic significance, social and environmental, also with respect to the national economy. Being the result of self-organisation processes and individuals' decisions, the boundaries of city-regions often do not correspond to existing administrative boundaries. This requires policy makers at various levels of government to co-ordinate in order to maximise the impact of their interventions on people's well-being, which is the ultimate objective of policy. In this respect, linking well-being metrics to the scale of cities can help the policy-making process, especially considering that – notwithstanding the fact that adopting a focus on people's outcome is at least as relevant for policy making at the local scale as it is at the national scale – most of the analyses of well-being are unconcerned with space and are carried out mostly at the national level.

This report identifies the major Danish city-regions and, subsequently, assesses their citizens' well-being in different dimensions of life. The different dimensions of life are assessed at various scales and levels of detail. The main idea of this report is that many of the factors affecting people's well-being come into play at the local scale, and city-regions represent one the most relevant geographies for people's daily life. Factors such as the conditions of the labour and housing markets, environmental quality, or the conditions in terms of personal safety and sense of community can change dramatically within a country and can be strictly linked to the specificities of the place where people live. This report follows the OECD Regional Well-being Framework, which identifies several dimensions of people's material conditions (income, jobs, housing) and quality of life (health, education, civic engagement, safety, access to services, environment, community and life satisfaction).

The five city-regions are compared in terms of the average outcomes experienced by their residents in each of the well-being dimensions analysed, but distinctions are also made with the rest of Denmark and with other countries' city-regions, when possible (Chapter 2). The report also analyses the dynamics that take place within each of the city-regions, at smaller geographies, such as that of the neighbourhood (Chapter 3). It distinguishes the core city from the commuting zone and it then tackles sub-municipal scales, providing measures of spatial segregation of the population by income and socio-economic status.

The indicators and evidence collected and produced in this report can be used for several purposes, according to the specific priorities and needs of policy makers and other stakeholders (i.e. citizens, institutions, economic actors). National policy makers, for example, can get a new perspective on differences in well-being across cities and between urban Denmark and the rest of the country, by using a common framework and metrics that allow for international comparisons. Local and city governments, on the other hand, can use this report to identify their relative strengths and weaknesses in well-being, to look at trends and compare them with those in other places. The indicators and the assessment provided can also help local policy makers initiate a discourse on the policy priorities and build a development strategy based on well-being metrics. In this respect, the report can provide a support for an effective prioritisation of interventions based on what matters the most for citizens. There are several examples in OECD countries – including in Denmark (Box 1.1) – where the measurement of well-being at the city, regional or local level represents the backbone of a new generation of policy which targets and engages people.

Identifying cities in Denmark

Administrative vs. functional cities and territorial reforms

Cities are continuing to attract population in both the developed and developing world, with consequences in terms of economy, environment and people's lifestyle. In the context of these urbanisation trends, the way cities are able to accommodate the coming together of people and economic activities can affect future economic prosperity and people's quality of life. However, monitoring urban development is not straightforward due to a lack of robust statistical information at city level for international comparisons. One of the most important challenges in this respect is the definition of the key concepts of urban development, such as that of a city and its boundaries.

A city can be measured using several approaches, including administrative, morphological and functional approaches. The administrative definition considers the boundaries of local governments (i.e. municipalities, counties, etc.) with population over a certain threshold as an approximation of cities. Despite the richness of statistical information on administrative units, this definition does not necessarily reflect the space individuals consider as the city in their daily activities. In addition, the administrative boundaries at the local level are seldom comparable across different countries. On the other hand, the morphological definition considers continuous urban settlements that reach a certain population size or density threshold. While this approach can allow international comparisons to be made, it tends to not be accurate in identifying the actual boundaries of cities, since it tends to take out all the areas having a lower density but being in all respects part of the city. Finally, according to a functional approach, a city is an economic and social entity composed of one or more dense urban cores to which a semi-rural or rural hinterland is functionally connected.

Box 1.1. **The Good Life initiative in Southern Denmark: Composite index vs. headline indicators**

The Region of Southern Denmark's vision embraces a wide spectrum of material and immaterial dimensions that are considered to contribute to a "Good Life". The multi-dimensionality of well-being was measured through two approaches successively: a composite index, which was eventually replaced with a dashboard of indicators. The Good Life was initially measured through a composite index encompassing five sub-indices: residents' health, security, relationships, self-fulfilment and surroundings. These five dimensions are considered to help enhance the chances of living the Good Life. Each of the sub-indices was measured using five socio-economic indicators and five indicators of perceived individual conditions. An exception was self-fulfilment, which was only measured by individual indicators.

Extensive discussions conducted by the region with each of the 22 municipalities indicated that the composite index was difficult to understand per se (the index was expressed as standard deviations and included variables at both individual and municipal level) and was not able to point out the exact areas in which policy intervention was required. The composite index was revised into a "wheel" that organises 40 indicators into 2 categories: community conditions (including a municipality profile and a citizen profile) and individuals' own perception of life.

Socio-economic indicators are measured using existing sources of data: registry data (indicators mainly available from the Statistics Denmark) and model data (from SAM-K/LINE, a regional version of the national ADAM economic model run by the Ministry of Finance, and the region's own geographic information system [GIS] analysis). Individual perception indicators are measured using panel survey data collected annually from up to 4 300 respondents (out of 1.2 million inhabitants). The region carries out citizen surveys three to four times per year. Once a year, citizens are asked to assess their level of well-being, both in general and in terms of different well-being dimensions, such as health, relationships, etc. The remaining surveys are dedicated to different themes regarding the Good Life and regional development. There is also an extensive national health survey "How are you?" ("*Hvordan har du det?*") which is run regionally every fourth year by the health department of the Region of Southern Denmark.

Source: OECD (2014a), *How's Life in Your Region? Measuring Regional and Local Well-being for Policy Making*, http://dx.doi.org/10.1787/9789264217416-en.

Despite the fact that people, information and goods are much more mobile than in the past, such enhanced mobility has not implied "the death of distance", but instead an ongoing process of urban concentration practically everywhere (Veneri, 2015) and an increase of the importance of geographic location. Moreover, cities are increasingly seen as providing the critical context to stimulate economic growth and contribute to prosperity (McCann, 2008). The reduction in transport costs has not yielded to a world where physical distance has no importance and where the concentration of people and economic activities in space is no longer relevant. It has instead led to the increasing importance of city-regions (Rodriguez-Pose, 2008) in understanding urban development across the world.

City boundaries tend to change according to the evolution of the economy and of the activities that are taken into account. Municipal boundaries – and in general the administrative structure of a country – are instead often stable over time and can remain unchanged for decades. When this happens, significant gaps between the functional boundaries of contemporary cities and the administrative structures that govern economic processes can occur. In the case of Denmark, these gaps were in part addressed through a reform of public administration which was fully implemented at the beginning of 2007. The reform provided the intermediate level of government (i.e. regions) with responsibility for healthcare and functions related to regional economic development, while municipalities were provided with functions of welfare services. The Danish reform of public administration also included a territorial reform leading to a significant reduction in the number of both regions and municipalities (Box 1.2).

Box 1.2. The Danish local government reform

The Danish government implemented a local government reform in 2007 based on three main pillars:

1. **A new map of Denmark.** The 14 counties existing before the reform were eliminated and replaced by 5 new regions (TL2). The number of municipalities was reduced from 271 to 98 through mergers, resulting in an average size of almost 56 000 inhabitants per municipality. Before the reform, the average size of municipalities was less than 20 000 inhabitants and nearly half of municipalities had less than 10 000. The reform also abolished the Greater Copenhagen authority created in 2000 and the same happened with the dual status of municipality and county that Copenhagen, Frederiksberg and Bornholm had before the reform. All three of these municipalities are now part of the Capital Region of Denmark.
2. **A new distribution of tasks between levels of government.** A number of tasks were transferred from the counties, leaving the municipalities responsible for handling most welfare tasks. Municipal responsibilities include: social services, child care, compulsory education, special education for adults, rehabilitation and long-term care for the elderly, preventive healthcare, nature and environmental planning, local business services, promotion of tourism, participation in regional transport companies, maintenance of the local road network, libraries, schools of music, local sports and cultural facilities, and a responsibility for employment that is shared with the central government.

   The new regions took over responsibility for healthcare from the counties, including hospitals and public health insurance covering general practitioners and specialists, pharmaceuticals, etc. The regions also have a number of tasks involving regional development.

   The central government was given a clearer role in overseeing efficiency in the provision of municipal and regional services. Employment services became a responsibility shared with municipalities, and responsibility for upper secondary schools was reallocated to the central government. Tax collection was also transferred to the central government, as well as part of collective transport and road maintenance and it assumed an increased role in nature and environmental planning. Finally, responsibility for culture was transferred to the central government (in practice, subsidising a number of private cultural institutions of national character).
3. **A new financial and equalisation system.** The number of taxation levels was reduced from three to two, since the regions, unlike the counties, no longer have the authority to impose taxes. Their revenues consist of block grants and activity-based funding from the central government and the municipalities. In addition, in order to ensure that the local government reform does not result in changes in the distribution of the cost burden between the municipalities, a reform of the grant and equalisation system was carried out, which takes into account the new distribution of tasks.

Source: Dexia (2008), *Subnational Governments in the European Union: Organisation, Responsibilities and Finance.*

A functional approach can be particularly appropriate to measure the boundaries of contemporary cities. Various socio-economic phenomena that characterised recent decades, such as, among others, long-lasting and still continuing urbanisation processes and improvements of communication and the transportation of people and goods requires considering socio-economic linkages – such as those of the labour market, consumption patterns or leisure – when measuring the boundaries of cities. Morphological and administrative boundaries often fail to account for such linkages.

Cities are defined in this report according to the method developed by the OECD (2012). Following this method, cities are intended as agglomerations composed of one or more dense urban cores and a surrounding semi-rural or rural commuting zone. This definition of city identifies what in both the scientific literature and policy practice is known as "city-regions" or "functional urban areas". Throughout this report, the terms city, city-region and functional urban area (FUA) are used interchangeably.

Redefining the boundaries of major Danish cities

The identification of city-regions can be relevant for both analytical and policy purposes. Analytically, it allows urbanisation to be monitored by considering cities in their economic meaning. In terms of policy, it helps identify the scale that should be taken into account when designing and implementing policy interventions that are relevant at the city level and that ultimately affect people's well-being, such as, among others, economic development, housing and transport. By considering the right scale, it is possible to maximise the effectiveness of policy by overcoming possible co-ordination problems associated with a fragmented governance structure and possible negative externalities generated by an excessive competition among contiguous municipalities.

Typically, labour market flows (daily trips from home to work) are used as the main proxy for the identification of city-regions. Such flows allow a wide set of linkages among people and businesses to be taken into account. In this respect, the United States (Berry, 1973), the United Kingdom (Coombes et al., 1979) and Italy (Istat-Irpet, 1989) were among the first countries to produce maps of "functional regions", from the perspective of commuting, covering the whole national territory.

There are several methods to identify cities according to their functional definition. The OECD, in collaboration with the EU, developed a method to identify functional city boundaries in a consistent way across countries (OECD, 2012). The method has been applied to 30 OECD countries and allows robust international comparative analysis to be performed on socio-economic phenomena at a consistent level of urban geography. The identification procedure is based on the idea that an FUA is composed of high-density cores and a surrounding commuting zone, which has a lower density, but which is highly connected to the core in terms of commuting flows (see Box 1.3 for a detailed description of the method).

Danish FUAs were identified by the OECD for the first time in 2012 by using 2001 data on population density and commuting flows (OECD, 2012). The current volume provides an updated identification by using 2011 population grid and commuting data. As a result, 5 FUAs of at least 50 000 inhabitants have been identified in Denmark and are represented in Figure 1.1. With respect to the previous identification, the FUA of Esbjerg has been added to the list. Additionally, Copenhagen appears as a polycentric city-region, since it contains two interconnected, but physically separated, urban cores.

Figure 1.1. **Cities in Denmark**

Source: OECD calculations based on LandScan data and 2011 census data and administrative boundaries.

It is worth acknowledging that the spatial boundaries of a city-region can easily extend beyond labour market areas, such as those identified through commuting flows. City-regions can be identified by considering different types of linkages, depending on the functions of most interest. The spatial extent of city-regions ends when linkages become weak, at the point where people do not share common resources, or carry out activities during their daily life. There are many types of linkages taking place in space that can be used to identify city-regions, such as the management of water sources, supply chains in agro-industry, tourism and innovation. Most of these processes are often associated with policy intervention at a broader scale than traditional labour market areas (OECD, 2013).

Basic socio-demographic characteristics of Danish cities

The five city-regions of Denmark concentrate 58% of the national population in the country in 2016, while they account for 61% of total employment. Among them, Copenhagen is the only city-region which, according to the OECD classification, can be defined as a "metropolitan area", since it had a population above 500 000 in 2011 – the year of reference for the identification of city boundaries. In 2016, Copenhagen accounted for 59% of the total urban population and 34% of the total population of Denmark, while the remaining cities together represent 24% of the total population in Denmark. Core cities in Denmark account for a large share of the population in the city-regions. Indeed, in 2015, 46% of the FUAs' population was concentrated in their core. This share ranges from 48% in Copenhagen to 42% in Aalborg.

Box 1.3. OECD method to identify functional urban areas

The OECD, in collaboration with the European Commission and Eurostat, has developed a method to define city-regions (or functional urban areas, FUAs) according to functional criteria and in a way that can be consistently applied across countries, in order to make international comparative analyses possible. Using population density and travel-to-work flows as key information, city-regions emerge as being characterised by densely inhabited "urban cores" (also called "cities") and less-populated municipalities whose labour market is highly integrated with the cores. The use of population grid data to identify urban cores compensates for the fact that traditional administrative units (e.g. municipalities or other geographical units used as building blocks) are unevenly sized and vary greatly within and between countries.

So far, the method has been applied to 30 OECD countries and a total of 1 197 functional urban areas have been identified where two-thirds of the OECD population lives. This method was first applied to Denmark using administrative boundaries and population grid data based on the 2001 census. As a result, four FUAs were identified in Denmark (Copenhagen, Aarhus, Odense and Aalborg). The method has been reapplied using new grid population and commuting data.

The method consists of three main steps:

1. identification of contiguous densely inhabited urban cores
2. identification of interconnected urban cores that are part of the same functional area
3. definition of the outlying area or commuting zone of the functional urban area, linked by commuting flows to the urban cores.

1. **Urban core.** The identification of urban cores can be divided in three steps, which are listed below.

- All grid cells from LandScan with a density of more than 1 500 inhabitants per km² are selected.
- High-density clusters are defined as aggregations of continuous high-density cells (which are sized 1 km² each). After having filled the gaps – cells entirely surrounded by high-density cells – only the clusters with a minimum population of 50 000 inhabitants are kept as high-density clusters.
- An urban core is made up of contiguous municipalities (based on 2011 boundaries) that have more than 50% of their populations living within "high-density" cells.

2. **Polycentric city.** Two urban cores are considered integrated and thus part of the same polycentric metropolitan system if more than 15% of the population of either of the cores commutes to work to the other core. Using such a definition, Copenhagen emerges as a polycentric FUA constituted of the urban core of the central city of Copenhagen with a large population nucleus and a smaller sub-centre, Vallensbæk, which has a high degree of integration with the nucleus.

3. **Commuting zone.** The final step of the methodology consists of delineating the commuting zone of the FUAs. The commuting zone can be defined as the "worker catchment area" of the urban labour market, outside the densely inhabited city. In order to delineate the extension of the commuting zone, municipalities (Local administrative units, LAU2) were assigned to each city if at least 15% of the population in the municipality travels to work to the central city.

Source: Author's analysis; OECD (2012), *Redefining "Urban": A New Way to Measure Metropolitan Areas*, http://dx.doi.org/10.1787/9789264174108-en.

During the last 15 years, population growth was stronger in city-regions than in the rest of Denmark (0.60% and 0.16% per year, respectively) (Table 1.1). However, the growth rate of population was not homogeneous across cities. Aarhus and Copenhagen, which are also the largest cities, are the ones which experienced the strongest growth, with an annual rate of 0.83% and 0.67%, respectively. Odense and Esbjerg, on the other hand, grew less than the national average (0.41% annually).

Table 1.1. **Basic socio-demographic characteristics of Danish cities**

City-region	Resident population (2016)	% population growth (annual rate) (2000-16)	Employed persons (2014)	% people over 65 years old (2016)	Δ in the share of people over 65 (pp) (2008-16)	% of foreign people (2016)
Copenhagen	1 921 869	0.67	1 010 529	16.5	2.1	11.3
Aarhus	501 795	0.83	248 397	15.9	3.0	7.5
Odense	376 496	0.33	162 349	19.4	3.4	6.7
Aalborg	313 978	0.45	143 702	18.5	2.9	6.3
Esbjerg	169 327	0.03	82 991	19.8	4.1	7.1
Rest of the country	2 423 786	0.16	1 071 872	42.3	4.5	6.3
Denmark	5 707 251	0.41	2 719 840	27.8	3.3	7.6

Note: Boundaries of city-regions are approximated to the closest municipal boundaries (see Annex 1.A1).

Source: Based on data from Statistics Denmark.

The most striking difference between the city-regions and the rest of the territory is in the structure of the population by age. Denmark is ageing, but cities concentrate most of the young population of the country. The share of people over 65 years old ranges from around 16% in Aarhus and Copenhagen to almost 20% in Esbjerg, while in non-urban places the share is 42.3%. Since 2008, the share of people over 65 years old has increased everywhere. However, the largest increase is observed outside city-regions (+4.5 pp) and in Esbjerg (+4.1 pp), while the lowest is in Copenhagen (+2.1 pp). This situation can challenge the capacity of providing and maintaining an adequate provision of services for elderly people, especially in more sparsely populated areas, where such provision can have higher costs due to weaker economies of scale.

The share of the population that is foreign-born is relatively low in Denmark compared with the OECD average (7.6% and 15.2% of total population, respectively).[1] The share of the foreign-born population in cities is in line with that of the rest of the country. The only exception is Copenhagen, where a relatively higher portion of the population is composed of migrants (11.3% in 2016). In this respect, a policy to increase the spatial dispersion of migrants has been recently introduced. However, such a measure tends to reduce geographical mobility and can be a barrier to both employment and to stronger networks for migrants (OECD, 2016a). In 2014, Denmark was the country with the fourth highest gap in employment rates between native-born and foreign-born workers (-10.3 pp versus +1.2 pp, respectively, in 2014), after Sweden, the Netherlands and Belgium. In addition, this gap tends to be transmitted across generations (OECD, 2016a: 35-37).

What approach to measure well-being in cities?

The measurement of well-being in Danish cities builds on the conceptual framework of the OECD Better Life Initiative and on the OECD *Regional Well-being Database* (OECD, 2014a). According to such a framework, well-being is a multi-dimensional concept. In order to provide a sound picture of the most relevant aspects of people's life, well-being measures should have a set of features. Such features include, among others, the fact that indicators should focus on outcome indicators, rather than only on input (e.g. resources spent on specific policies, such as new staff, infrastructure, etc.) or output (e.g. the efficiency of policy given the input invested) indicators. Outcome indicators focus on the actual conditions experienced by people, which is also the ultimate objective of policy, although they are typically only indirectly affected by policy makers. Second, and when possible given data constraints, indicators should be informative of both average living conditions and of the distribution of such conditions across places and groups of the population. Third, the measurement of well-being is multidimensional and accounts for both material conditions and quality of life. Finally, well-being measures should include and combine both objective and subjective indicators. The joint consideration of both types of measure ensures that individual characteristics and those of the communities where people live are accounted for in the measurement of well-being through an approach focused on people.

Based on these considerations, the OECD published in 2014 *How's Life in Your Region?*, which provided a framework (Figure 1.2) and a database to measure well-being at the subnational level, in all 395 regions of the OECD, where regions generally correspond to the first tier of subnational government. The new version of the database[2] covers 11 well-being dimensions and includes also self-reported experience of well-being, such as sense of community and satisfaction with life. Well-being outcomes can be improved by policy and change relies on the role played by citizenship, institutions and governance. Moreover, a focus on place allows the interactions between well-being dimensions to be better accounted for. Such interactions should be reflected in the policy design at the local level, which should try to build on the complementarities and to manage the existing trade-offs, which are likely to be most evident where they happen, in specific places.

Figure 1.2. **The regional well-being conceptual framework**

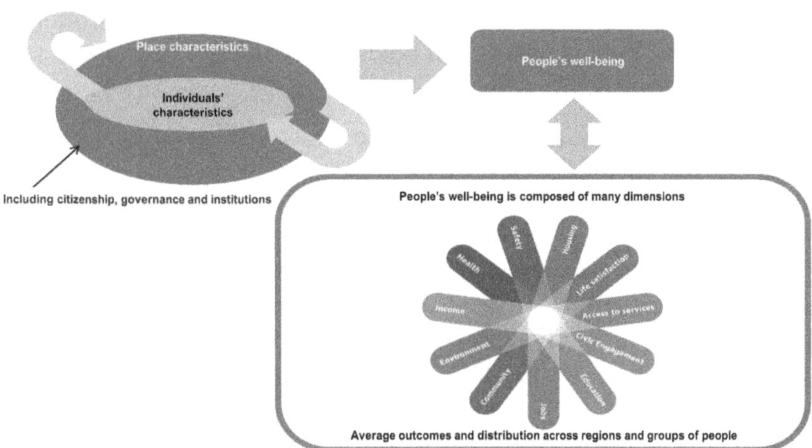

Source: OECD (2014a), *How's Life in Your Region? Measuring Regional and Local Well-being for Policy Making*, http://dx.doi.org/10.1787/9789264217416-en.

The potential use of subnational well-being metrics for policy making has stimulated several regions and cities to launch initiatives integrating well-being measurement in policy design and monitoring. The seven case studies in *How's Life in Your Region?* (OECD, 2014a) document this type of experience. For example, the Region of Southern Denmark promoted an initiative called "The Good Life" (see Box 1.1) to measure well-being in all municipalities and help policy makers identify areas for policy prioritisation, raise social awareness and improve policy coherence across different policy domains (OECD, 2014b). Similarly, the state of Morelos (Mexico) introduced a large set of well-being indicators to set targets within its multi-year State Development Plan (OECD, 2014c). Inspired by this type of initiative, the OECD produced a report in late 2015 and a data visualisation tool to measure well-being in all Mexican states and use such indicators in the design and implementation of policy (OECD, 2015).

One key feature of people's well-being is that it can be affected by the place where individuals live. Some of the aspects that matter for people's life, such as the environmental quality, the level of safety of the area, accessibility to services, the conditions of the labour market or the sense of community, can change dramatically according to the place where one lives. This can happen not only within the same country, but also within the same region or city. Geographically detailed data and indicators add important information that can be used to understand how advantages or disadvantages in well-being dimensions are distributed not only among different groups of people, but also across locations.

In the case of Denmark, well-being outcomes are generally high in practically all dimensions of life. When assessed at the regional scale, people's well-being shows relatively low disparities compared with other OECD countries on almost all well-being dimensions (OECD, 2016b). However, a more geographically detailed perspective can provide new insights and a more nuanced picture of the actual conditions of people in the place where they live and work. This report represents a further step in this direction, since it goes beyond the regional scale to focus on cities. This more detailed approach allows well-being to be accounted for at a scale that is more coherent with people's everyday life and helps identify the areas of policy where improvement is needed. A more precise and detailed measurement can also stimulate a constructive and more informed dialogue among citizens, policy makers and other stakeholders who want to take actions towards better lives.

The focus on cities makes it possible also to cover issues that are specific to the urban scale, such as the way people locate in different neighbourhoods according to their income or other socio-economic or cultural characteristics, or the different conditions in terms of quality of life between central urban locations and more peripheral ones at the outskirt of cities. This report addresses many of these aspects, by looking at differences between the well-being of people living in the cores of cities with respect to those living in the commuting zones. In addition, it analyses which areas of the cities are attracting more population, as well as the patterns of spatial segregation by income within the different neighbourhoods of cities and how the job market conditions change across neighbourhoods.

The focus on cities requires some adaptations of the Regional Well-being Framework, especially due to statistical challenges. Building well-being indicators that are sound and comparable across countries requires overcoming the challenges of the production of statistics at the city level. Several indicators of well-being at the national level are typically computed from household surveys (i.e. income levels and inequality) which, however, are rarely designed to be representative below the national or the regional scale. These constraints can be overcome in different ways, including performing small area estimation techniques or combining survey data with other sources of data that are available at a small geographical scale, such as census data. Another solution consists of using non-survey sources of data, such as administrative data, which can have a more detailed geographic availability. Building on the recent OECD work to measure income levels and inequality in metropolitan areas (OECD, 2016c), this report makes use of administrative data provided by the Statistics Denmark and the Region of Southern Denmark to compute statistics at the city level on many dimensions of well-being. Other possible options consist in making use of GIS, especially when global cartographies make international comparisons possible. The estimation of $PM_{2.5}$ at city level presented in the report builds on this type of data. Using big data also represents a promising solution at the local level, since it allows already existing and timely information to be exploited to produce information at the desired geography (OECD, 2016c).

What this report offers

Chapter 2 provides an assessment of well-being outcomes across the major Danish cities. The indicators used in the report cover 11 well-being dimensions, which are jobs, income, housing, accessibility to services, education, health, civic engagement and governance, environment, safety, social connections, and life satisfaction. The chapter describes trends and patterns of well-being across cities and highlights the differences between the living conditions in the most central and dense areas – the city cores – and their surrounding low-density hinterland which is connected to the cores – the commuting zones.

The results highlight that large cities often have different living conditions with respect to the rest of the country. People living in Copenhagen, the only Danish "metropolitan area" – a city-region of more than 500 000 inhabitants – have on average an income which is 15% higher than those living in other locations of the country. Household income in the two largest Danish cities – Copenhagen and Aarhus – has been growing faster than in the other cities since 2000. Income inequality has been growing as well, especially driven by the higher growth in the income of the most affluent households with respect to the less affluent ones.

While people living in cities have, on average, higher income levels and educational attainment, they have relatively less safety and social support with respect to those living elsewhere. However, people's well-being is not homogenous within cities. Life expectancy, for example, can vary significantly according to the municipality of residence, and it tends to be higher in larger and more affluent ones. Income levels are relatively higher in the commuting zone than in the city core. Similarly, unemployment and crime – despite being relatively low compared with most OECD countries – are also not homogeneous within cities and tend to be increasingly concentrated in the city cores.

Chapter 3 describes in more detail the patterns of well-being within each city, by considering issues of population growth, spatial segregation of people by income, concentration of unemployment and youth unemployment up to the scale of the neighbourhood. The chapter highlights that in the last ten years population has grown faster in the largest parishes[3] and in those closer to the main urban centres. Population in the commuting zones of Danish cities has been ageing faster than that in the city-core since 2008.

Danish cities have experienced an increase in income inequality since the early 2000s and this might have affected current patterns of spatial segregation by income – i.e. the concentration of people with similar income in different neighbourhoods of the city. Notwithstanding the fact that levels of spatial segregation are relatively low in Danish cities with respect to those in other OECD countries, low-income households are those which tend to concentrate the most in specific neighbourhoods (OECD, 2016d). This is somewhat different from what happens in other countries, such as Canada, France and the United States, where the most affluent are those with the highest tendency to cluster.

When assessed in terms of employment status, spatial segregation tends to be higher in the city cores than in the commuting zone of Danish cities, with the exception of Copenhagen. On the other hand, hot spots of youth unemployment can be observed in Denmark, especially in Aalborg and in the region of Copenhagen, but outside the boundaries of the city-region.

Finally, Chapter 4 provides a short summary on the challenges and way forward in using well-being measures in policy making at the local or city scale. It also present some examples of initiatives carried out in Danish regions and municipalities where a well-being framework was adopted.

How can the results of this report be used?

This report provides a comprehensive picture of people's well-being in the major Danish cities. It can be used primarily by local policy makers who want to better understand the well-being of their citizens through a metrics of outcomes indicators which can help design a development strategy and prioritise policy interventions where improvement is most required. The evidence provided in the report can also help initiate a discourse with citizens to raise awareness on the actual living conditions in the different cities and across their different neighbourhoods in order to identify the policy domains where change is needed the most.

The report can also be used by national policy makers to monitor urban development and how the latter translates into the well-being of people living in contemporary cities. The report allows sound comparisons to be made with other cities across the OECD, thanks to the use of a consistent definition of cities based on the actual behaviour of people rather than on administrative boundaries and using similar indicators following the OECD approach to measuring well-being at the subnational level.

Making indicators of well-being available at a small spatial scale, as recently done by Statistics Denmark, is crucial to advance in the measurement of well-being at the local scale and to help the policy-making process at all levels of government. The use of administrative sources of data and of a geographical information system is very important to further improve the measurement of people's living conditions at detailed geographies.

Notes

1. The OECD average refers to 2013 (source: *OECD Migration Database* https://data.oecd.org/migration/foreign-born-population.htm), while the figure for Denmark refers to 2016 (source: Statistics Denmark).
2. Available at: www.oecdregionalwellbeing.org.
3. A parish in Denmark is an ecclesiastical community. Until the municipal reform of 1970, parishes were an administrative territorial unit. Even in the present day, the original parish boundaries still play a significant role, for example in determining community boundaries and school districts.

References

Berry, B.J.L. (1973), *Growth Centers in the American Urban System*, Bollinger, Cambridge, Massachusetts.

Coombes, M.G. et al. (1979), "Daily urban systems in Britain: From theory to practice", *Environment and Planning A*, Vol. 11/5, pp. 565-574, http://dx.doi.org/10.1068/a110565.

Dexia (2008), *Subnational Governments in the European Union: Organisation, Responsibilities and Finance*, Dexia Editions, Paris.

Istat-Irpet (1989), *I Mercati Locali del Lavoro*, Franco Angeli, Milan, Italy.

McCann, P. (2008), "Globalization and economic geography: The world is curved, not flat", *Cambridge Journal of Regions Economy and Society*, Vol. 1/3, pp. 351-370, http://dx.doi.org/10.1093/cjres/rsn002.

OECD (2016a), *OECD Economic Surveys: Denmark 2016*, OECD Publishing, Paris, http://dx.doi.org/10.1787/eco_surveys-dnk-2016-en.

OECD (2016b), *OECD Regions at a Glance 2016*, OECD Publishing, Paris, http://dx.doi.org/10.1787/reg_glance-2016-en.

OECD (2016c), "Measuring housing purchasing power parities at regional level: A hedonic approach using web-scraped data", OECD, Paris.

OECD (2016d), *Making Cities Work for All: Data and Actions for Inclusive Growth*, OECD Publishing, Paris, http://dx.doi.org/10.1787/9789264263260-en.

OECD (2015), *Measuring Well-being in Mexican States*, OECD Publishing, Paris, http://dx.doi.org/10.1787/9789264246072-en.

OECD (2014a), *How's Life in Your Region?: Measuring Regional and Local Well-being for Policy Making*, OECD Publishing, Paris, http://dx.doi.org/10.1787/9789264217416-en.

OECD (2014b), "Region of Southern Denmark (Denmark)", in: *How's Life in Your Region?: Measuring Regional and Local Well-being for Policy Making*, OECD Publishing, Paris, http://dx.doi.org/10.1787/9789264217416-8-en.

OECD (2014c), "State of Morelos (Mexico)", in: *How's Life in Your Region?: Measuring Regional and Local Well-being for Policy Making*, OECD Publishing, Paris, http://dx.doi.org/10.1787/9789264217416-11-en.

OECD (2013), *Rural-Urban Partnerships: An Integrated Approach to Economic Development*, OECD Publishing, Paris, http://dx.doi.org/10.1787/9789264204812-en.

OECD (2012), *Redefining "Urban": A New Way to Measure Metropolitan Areas*, OECD Publishing, Paris, http://dx.doi.org/10.1787/9789264174108-en.

OECD (2011), *How's Life? Measuring Well-being*, OECD Publishing, Paris, http://dx.doi.org/10.1787/9789264121164-en.

Rodríguez-Pose, A. (2008), "The rise of the 'city-region' concept and its development policy implications", *European Planning Studies*, Vol. 16/8, pp. 1 025-1 046, http://dx.doi.org/10.1080/09654310802315567.

Veneri, P. (2015), "Urban spatial structure in OECD cities: Is urban population decentralising or clustering?", *OECD Regional Development Working Papers*, No. 2015/01, OECD Publishing, Paris, http://dx.doi.org/10.1787/5js3d834r3q7-en.

Annex 1.A1.
Cities in Denmark approximated to the closest municipal boundaries

For some well-being dimensions (see Table 2.A1.1 in Annex 2.A1 for details) data are available at the municipal level. This implies that the corresponding indicators for the city-regions do not refer to the exact boundaries of city-regions as identified in Figure 1.1, since the latter have been adjusted to the closest municipal boundaries. In these cases, the resulting boundaries of city-regions are those represented in Figure 1.A1.1. Differences in terms of total resident population in 2016 range from 3% in the case of Copenhagen to 22% in the case of Esbjerg.

Figure 1.A1.1. **Cities in Denmark approximated to the closest municipal boundaries**

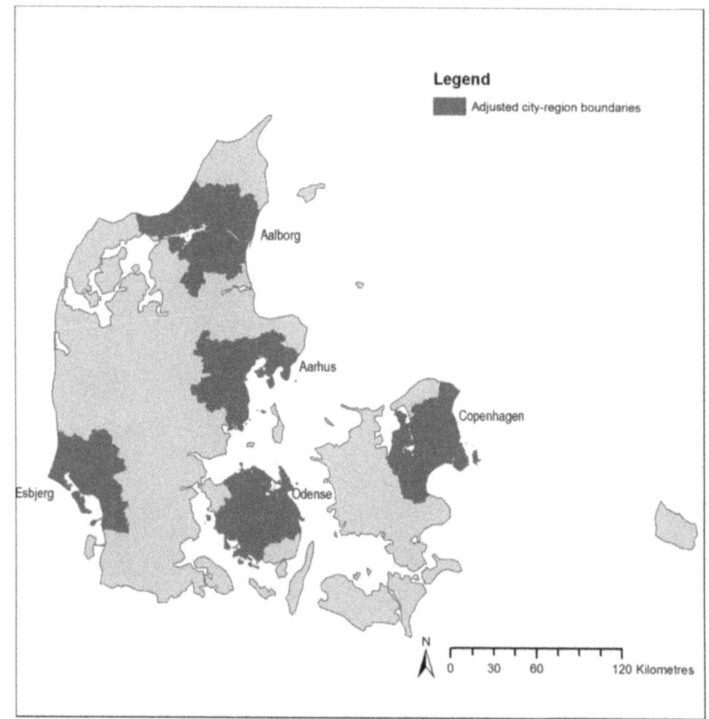

Source: OECD calculations based on LandScan data and 2011 census data and administrative boundaries.

Table 1.A1.1. **Number of municipalities and parishes within Danish cities**

City-region	Number of municipalities	Number of parishes
Copenhagen	31	247
Aarhus	5	109
Odense	6	109
Aalborg	4	78
Esbjerg	3	40

Note: A parish in Denmark is an ecclesiastical community. Until the municipal reform of 1970, parishes were an administrative territorial unit. Even in the present day, the original parish boundaries still play a significant role, for example in determining community boundaries and school districts

Chapter 2.

The geography of well-being in Danish cities

This chapter provides an assessment of levels and trends of people's well-being in the five major Danish cities, namely Copenhagen, Aarhus, Aalborg, Esbjerg and Odense. Cities are defined according to the OECD definition of functional urban areas and are composed of a high-density core and a commuting zone. Indicators cover 11 well-being dimensions, following the OECD Regional Well-being Framework. The different outcomes between core and commuting zone are highlighted and discussed and, when possible, outcomes are compared with those in other cities of the OECD. The chapter also presents levels and trends of income inequality within Danish cities.

Introduction

This chapter provides an assessment of people's well-being in the five major Danish cities. It describes both levels and trends of various indicators in 11 dimensions of life that include both material conditions such as income, jobs and housing, as well as quality of life dimensions, such as access to services, health, safety, education, environment, civic engagement, social connections and life satisfaction. All of the indicators used in this chapter to compare well-being outcomes across Danish cities are summarised in Table 2.1.

Table 2.1. **Dimensions and indicators to measure well-being in Danish cities**

Dimension	Indicator
Income	Equivalised household disposable income
	Gini coefficient of household disposable income (inequality)
Jobs	Unemployment rate
	Labour participation rate
	Part-time employment
Housing	Rooms per person
	Square metres per person*
	Housing costs
	Proportion of tenant occupied housing
Access to services	Number of full-time jobs accessible by car within 30 and 60 minutes
Safety	Homicide rate
	Reported criminal offences
Education	Share of working-age population with a tertiary education
	Score in Danish, English and mathematics*
Environment	Air pollution: concentration of $PM_{2.5}$ in µg/m^3
	Distance to highly valued natural amenities
Civic engagement	Voter turnout
Health	Life expectancy
	Total hospital admissions
	Uncontrolled hospital admissions for diabetes mellitus
Community (social connections)	Lack of social support
	Feeling of loneliness*
Life satisfaction	Satisfaction with life (on a scale from 0 to 100)*

* Indicators available only for the cities in the Region of Southern Denmark (Esbjerg and Odense).

The choice of dimensions and indicators is primarily based on the OECD Better Life Framework and on the OECD Regional Well-being Framework (see Chapter 1), which underwent a long process of consultation across national statistical offices and other stakeholders in OECD countries to agree on the way to measure well-being for international comparisons. With respect to the OECD Better Life Framework, this report presents indicators in all dimensions except the one on work-life balance, for reasons of data availability, though it is worth noting that, at the national level, Denmark ranks second among OECD countries with its score in this dimension. The assessment of well-being in cities brings about specific statistical challenges that make it difficult to adopt exactly the same indicators normally used at the national or regional level. Some indicators presented and discussed in this report are not included in the OECD Regional Well-being Framework and have been included here based on relevant issues for Denmark's policy agenda at the scale of cities. Examples include social inclusion (i.e. spatial segregation by income and jobs outcomes), labour participation and other subjective indicators such as the feeling of loneliness or the highly valued natural amenities. Data sources are of different types, including the most geographically detailed grid-level data at one or two points in time, municipal data provided by Statistics Denmark and subsequently aggregated at the geography of cities and survey data, such as in the case of the subjective well-being indicators for the cities of the Region of Southern Denmark (see Annex 2.A1).

The full set of indicators provided in this chapter can constitute a useful base to identify – through a city lens – specific dimensions where improvement is most needed and to monitor progress over time. It also opens the way to analyse how well-being is distributed spatially within different parts of the cities, covering issues such as spatial segregation by income, occupational status and youth unemployment. These issues will be analysed more in detail in Chapter 3. Finally, the assessment provided in this chapter also allows the most relevant statistical challenges to be identified in order to measure well-being at a geographically detailed scale, such as the difficulties in using survey data and the need to further increase the availability of administrative data (i.e. income, jobs, education, etc.) at the municipal or at the small territorial grid scale. Similar challenges might exist also in other countries interested in monitoring how their cities perform through a well-being metrics. This report can also represent a useful illustration in this respect.

How Danish cities fare on the different well-being dimensions?

Income

In most developed and developing countries, cities are places that constantly attract people and economic activities from other locations. People moving to cities are often looking for opportunities to develop and to improve their material conditions and quality of life. The level of income available to households and individuals is a key indicator of people's material conditions, since it determines the amount of goods and services that can be purchased according to one's needs and preferences. In this report, income is measured in terms of household disposable income, which is defined as the sum of income deriving from employment, property, production of household services for own consumption and current transfers received (i.e. pensions, social benefits, etc.) minus current transfers paid (taxes, fees, social contributions, etc.). Such a measure is expressed per household and is comparable across countries having different taxation schemes.[1] On average in the OECD, households living in metropolitan areas – cities with more than 500 000 inhabitants – have levels of income that are 18% higher than those living elsewhere (Boulant, Brezzi and Veneri, 2016).[2] Such difference is lower in Denmark, where households living in Copenhagen, the only "metropolitan area" in the country, had incomes that are only 15% higher than in the rest of Denmark in 2014, suggesting a more balanced level of development across space than in most OECD countries.

Among Danish city-regions, Copenhagen had the highest average income per household in 2014, followed by Aarhus, Esbjerg, Aalborg and Odense (Figure 2.1). Odense is the only city-region where household incomes are, on average, lower than in non-urban Denmark. However, it is important to acknowledge that higher incomes in metropolitan areas do not necessarily translate into higher purchasing power for households, as differences in income levels can be, at least partially, offset by differences in living costs across space (World Bank, 2015).

Figure 2.1. **Equivalised household disposable income in Danish cities**

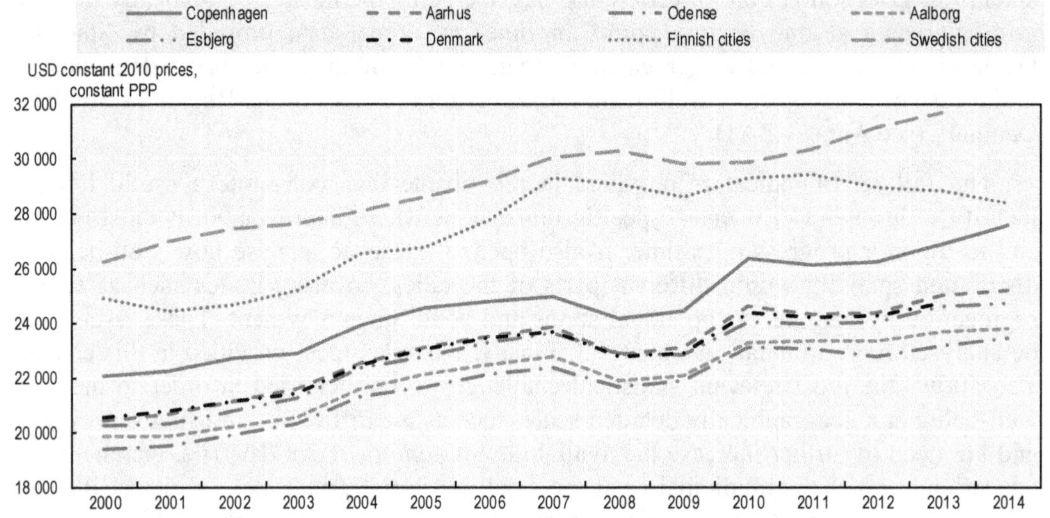

Note: Boundaries of city-regions are approximated to the closest municipal boundaries.

Source: OECD elaborations based on data from Statistics Denmark.

Income has grown in all city-regions since 2000. Aarhus and Copenhagen were the two best performing city-regions, with an average annual growth rate of 1.5% and 1.6%, respectively, between 2000 and 2014. Copenhagen was by far the top performing city in terms of income growth in the period after the economic crisis (2007-14), with an income growth of 1.42% per year. In all the other city-regions yearly growth rates of income ranged between 0.64% (Aalborg) and 0.8% (Aarhus), while outside cities and in the whole of Denmark income growth was on average 0.67% and 1.21% per year, respectively.

While large cities have on average higher incomes than smaller cities or other non-urban locations, they have higher inequality too. According to estimations based on administrative data provided by Statistics Denmark, Copenhagen is the Danish city with the highest Gini coefficient for household income in 2014 in Denmark (0.283), followed by Aarhus (0.260), Odense (0.228), Aalborg (0.227) and Esbjerg (0.221), while the national average was 0.240.[3] On the whole, household income is fairly equally distributed in Denmark with respect to other developed countries. According to the OECD *Income Distribution Database*, Denmark was the country with the lowest Gini coefficient in the OECD in 2013. Similar findings emerge when looking at the largest cities, with Copenhagen being among those with the lowest Gini coefficient, together with Oslo and Austrian cities (Boulant, Brezzi and Veneri, 2016).

Notwithstanding relatively low levels of inequality in Danish cities with respect to the OECD average, inequality has grown in the last 15 years, especially since the late 2000s, so that inclusiveness issues feature high on the national and subnational policy agendas. The rise in inequality is mostly explained by a faster income growth for households in the upper tail of the distribution with respect to the income of those in the lowest tail. This trend is reflected in all city-regions in Denmark and is also consistent with the overall trend of rising inequality in OECD countries (OECD, 2015a). Figure 2.2 shows changes between 2000 and 2014 in the average incomes of households in the top 20% and bottom 20% of the income distribution for the five Danish city-regions. While income of households in the bottom 20% increased by 15-16% in all city-regions, income growth of households in the top 20% of the income distribution ranged from 25% in Odense to 31% in Aarhus (28% on average). Behind this trend, both global and domestic processes that have been taking place in the last years might have played a role. Globally, the skill-biased technological change is a change in the production technology connected to the rapid rise in the relative earnings of skilled workers with respect to those of their more unskilled counterparts (Violante, 2008). More specific to the Danish situation are the domestic reforms put in place in recent years by the national government to foster economic growth, which relaxed the degree of social protection with possible positive effects on income inequality (OECD, 2016a), the increasing number of single-parent households (OECD, 2011) and the increase of capital income for the most affluent households (Ministry of Finance, 2015).

Figure 2.2. **Change in top 20% and bottom 20% of income in Danish cities**

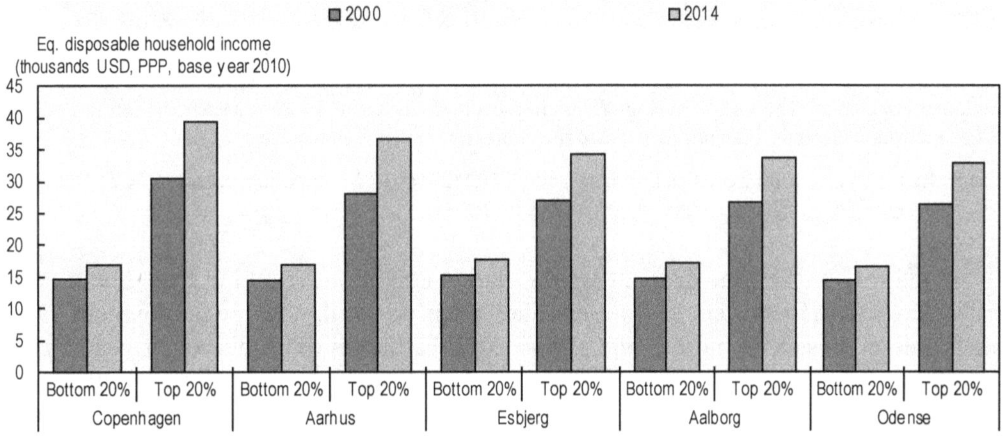

Note: Boundaries of city-regions are approximated to the closest municipal boundaries.

Source: Based on data from Statistics Denmark.

Jobs

A high participation in the labour market is crucial to maintain a generous welfare system. Recent structural reforms implemented in Denmark, such as the pension reform to reduce early retirement schemes, are expected to increase labour force participation and to compensate the pressures due to the ageing population (OECD, 2016a). Indeed, the labour participation rate in Denmark is lower today compared to before 2008, while the unemployment rate increased from less than 4% in 2008 to 6.3% in 2015. The decline in labour participation that has occurred in recent years might also be a rebound from a fast growth of the Danish economy during the decade prior to the start of the economic crisis of 2008. Figure 2.3 shows that Danish cities have higher participation rates than the OECD average of metropolitan areas.[4] However, the drop in the labour force participation rate was heterogeneous across Danish city-regions. In Copenhagen, where participation is the highest, the reduction was the lowest, while Odense has experienced an ongoing reduction in the participation of the working-age population in the labour market since 2008 (a 4-percentage point reduction over the period 2008-14). The participation rate in Odense stood at 74% in 2014, below 79% and 78% found in Copenhagen and in "non-urban" Denmark respectively. A similar gap exists between the participation rate in Aalborg and Aarhus and that in the rest of Denmark.

Figure 2.3. **Labour force participation rate in Danish cities**

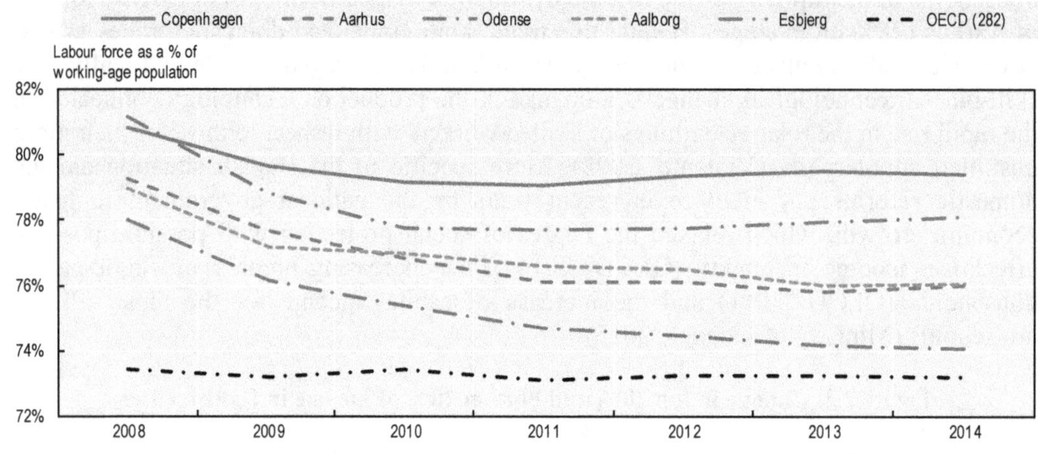

Notes: The labour force participation rate equals employment plus unemployment as a percentage of the working-age population (15-64 years old). Boundaries of city-regions are approximated to the closest municipal boundaries. The OECD average refers to the simple mean of the labour participation rate across all OECD metropolitan areas. Parenthesis indicate the number of metropolitan areas.

Source: Based on data from Statistics Denmark and OECD (2016d), "Metropolitan areas", *OECD Metropolitan Database*, https://stats.oecd.org/Index.aspx?DataSetCode=CITIES.

In many countries, the difficult labour market conditions resulting from the economic crisis have been persistent in metropolitan areas as well. The unemployment rate in metropolitan areas rose more in the period 2008-12 than it did in the eight years prior to that in 26 of the 28 OECD countries for which data was available (OECD, 2016b). Job markets in the vast majority of cities recorded deteriorations compared to December 2009. While unemployment declines are a positive sign for the nation's economy, full recovery from job losses after the crisis is a long way off in all functional urban areas, where the unemployment rate remains higher than it was in 2008. Esbjerg leads the Danish nation with an unemployment rate of 3% as of December of 2014 while the weakest – although compared with OECD standards still very strong – job market among the nation's FUAs is Aalborg with an unemployment rate of 4.7%.

Unemployment rates in the cores of Danish city-regions are always higher than in the commuting zones (Figure 2.4). Since 2003, improvements in terms of job outcomes were not homogeneous within the Southern city-regions: in both Esbjerg and Odense labour market conditions in the city cores deteriorated compared to that in their respective commuting zones. This trend was particularly strong in Esbjerg, where between 2003 and 2013 the unemployment rate in the core increased from 5% to 6%, while it remained stable at 3% in the commuting zone.

Trends in employment are similar: employment rates were lower in 2014 than six years prior to that and Odense is the city-region that had the most important decrease while Esbjerg the smallest one. However, quality of jobs has to be taken into account when considering employment trends. Compared to US employees, for example, Danish people tend to prefer working shorter hours and tend to adjust their working time according to their preferences in a time span of a decade, on average (Bonke and Schultz-Nielsen, 2016). In Esbjerg, the proportion of the workforce aged between 15 and 64 years old reporting that their main job was part-time increased from 27% in 2009 to 30% in 2011 (Figure 2.5). Still, the highest proportion of part-time workers in 2014 was found in

Odense followed by Aarhus, where part-time work accounted in each case for around a third of those in employment. By contrast, part-time employment in Copenhagen was significantly lower than in the rest of the country (26% of employed people).

Figure 2.4. **Ratio between the unemployment rate in the Danish cities cores and in the commuting zones**

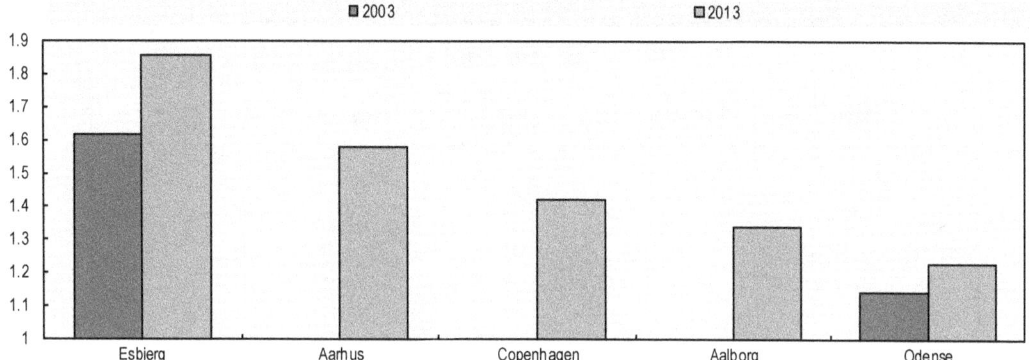

Note: Data for the year 2003 are only available for the city-regions in the Region of Southern Denmark.

Source: Based on data provided by the Region of Southern Denmark.

Figure 2.5. **Share of part-time employment in overall employment in Danish cities**

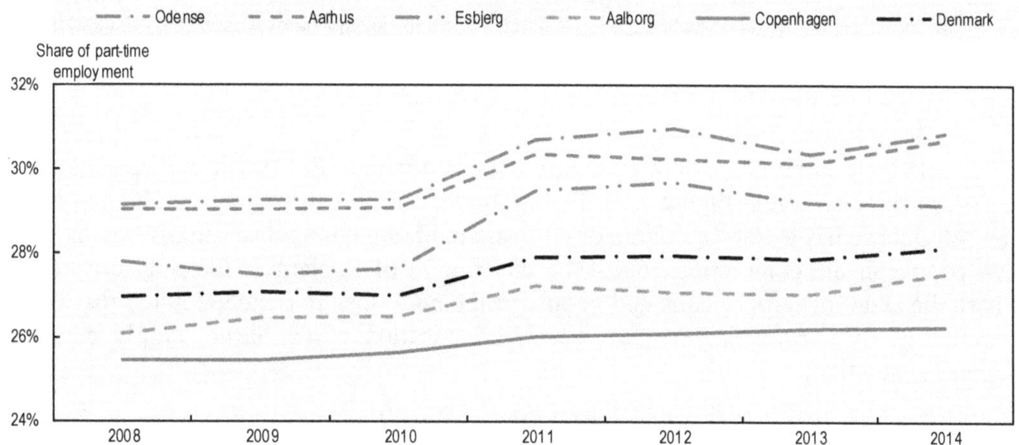

Note: Boundaries of city-regions are approximated to the closest municipal boundaries. Data adapted to the municipal boundaries definition of the city-regions.

Source: Based on data from Statistics Denmark.

Education

All Danish city-regions experienced an increase in the share of their youth and adults enrolled in tertiary education between 2006 and 2015 (Figure 2.6). Tertiary education provided by universities and other higher education institutions has a crucial role in fostering the progress of society. It also enhances innovation, increasing economic development and improving more generally the well-being of citizens. The largest increase in tertiary educational attainment (22%) occurred in the older industrial city-region of Aalborg, suggesting a transformation in the composition of the labour force of the city towards higher skills. Throughout the rest of the country over the same time span, more people are also going to college or graduate school. Nevertheless, as it happens also in most OECD countries, the major cities concentrate the largest part of the workforce with the highest educational attainments. In 2015, 41% and 42% of the working-age population had a tertiary education in Copenhagen and Aarhus, respectively, while outside cities the share was only 26%.

Figure 2.6. **Share of the working-age population (25-64 years old) with a tertiary education in Danish cities**

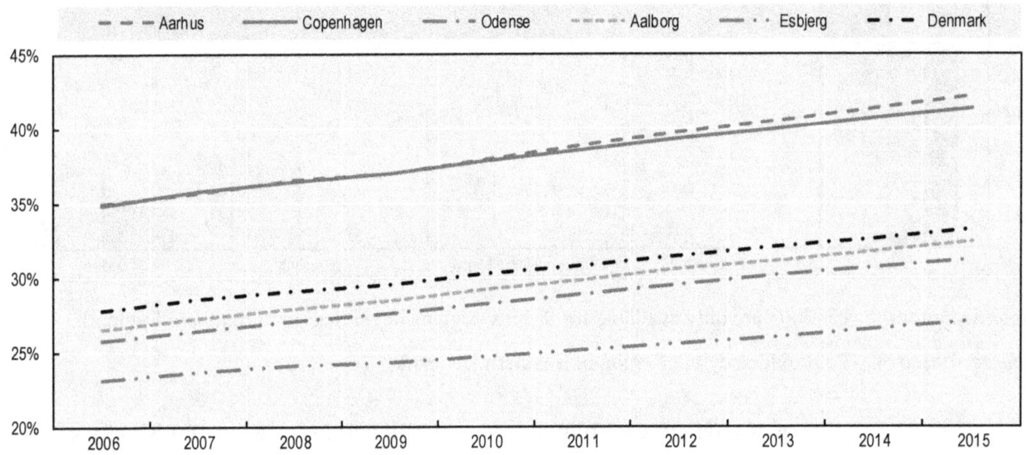

Note: Tertiary education includes Bachelor, Master and Doctoral levels and short-cycle tertiary education. Data are adapted to the closest municipal boundaries of the city-regions.

Source: Based on data from Statistics Denmark.

A relatively large proportion of highly educated people in Danish city-regions tends to sort in the city cores (Figure 2.7). For example, one in every three inhabitants in the core of Odense has a college degree or equivalent attainment against almost one in every five people in the commuting zone. The city-region of Esbjerg is the only city-region where the share of tertiary educated people in the core does not exceed much that of the commuting zone, reflecting in part the suburbanisation of the large, highly educated boomer generation.

While cities everywhere are increasing the skills of their workforce, progress appears to be relatively faster among the residents in the cores. The share of youth and adults living in cores and holding a college degree rose from 35% to 42% from 2006 to 2015, while a lower increase occurred in the commuting zones (from 29% to 33%).[5] This confirms a trend towards greater disparities between cores and commuting zones in terms of tertiary educational attainment. The largest increase in the core-commuting zone gap in terms of educational attainment occurred in Copenhagen and Esbjerg, which had the smallest disparities at the beginning of the period.

A wide range of literature demonstrates the importance of educational outcomes in childhood and youth to well-being as adults (OECD, 2015b). Understanding childhood educational outcomes, therefore, can be useful in identifying where improvement is needed and on which opportunities to build the future of young people. This issue does not cover a small part of the population: children and young people between 11 and 19 years old represent about 13% of total population in the OECD (OECD, 2015d). One possible indicator to measure the skills of young people in Danish cities is the test scores for ninth graders in Danish, English and mathematics (Table 2.2). In Denmark, ninth grade is the year of the first final exams, and the last year of "*Folkeskolen*" (the first ten years of education). The students are 15-16 years old and the age spectrum covered is only one point in late childhood. It is then not possible to assess educational achievement across a child's life cycle. Nonetheless, this timing in a child's life cycle means that accumulated learning from a compulsory school career is well represented by it. In all OECD countries, by the time a child reaches age 15, a considerable amount of government investment has been spent on a child's education.

Figure 2.7. **Share of the working-age population (25-64 years old) with a tertiary education in the Danish cities cores and commuting zones, 2013**

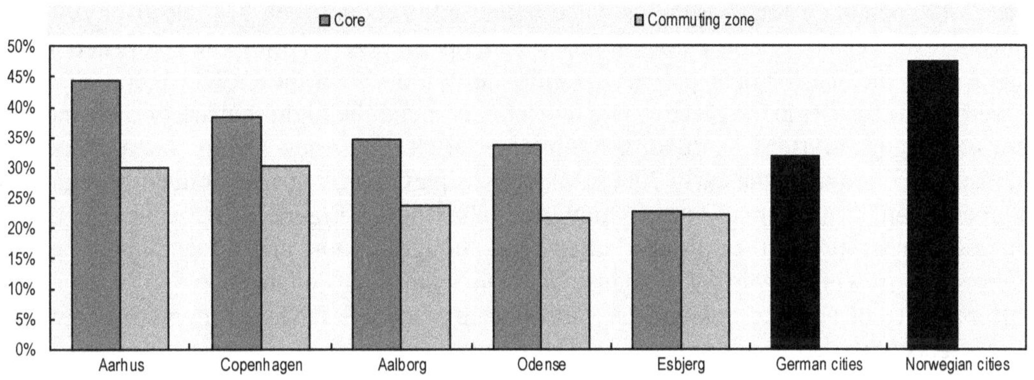

Note: Values for German and Norwegian cities refer to the average of the respective cities in 2012, without distinguishing cores and commuting zones.

Source: Based on data provided by the Region of Southern Denmark and OECD (2016d), "Metropolitan areas", *OECD Metropolitan Database*, https://stats.oecd.org/Index.aspx?DataSetCode=CITIES.

Table 2.2. **Scores of ninth graders in cities in the Region of Southern Denmark**

	Danish	English	Mathematics
Esbjerg – Core	6.4	7.4	6.6
Esbjerg – Commuting zone	6.8	7.7	7.2
Odense – Core	6.7	7.2	6.5
Odense – Commuting zone	6.7	7.3	6.9
Rest of the Region of Southern Denmark	6.7	7.3	6.9

Note: The scores are derived from mean scores for each municipality aggregated by city-region (based on all children living in the municipality, i.e. both public and private schools).

Source: Based on data provided by the Region of Southern Denmark.

Previous works have demonstrated that low-income students tend to underperform as students when compared to their counterparts coming from more affluent households (Dahl and Lochner, 2012). Student scores, especially in mathematics, are always higher for children attending schools in the commuting zones compared to those in the cores. Students living in the commuting zone of Esbjerg particularly stand out by their high scores in English and mathematics. These patterns are consistent with the findings highlighted in the previous sections that relatively more affluent households tend to concentrate in the commuting zones of the Danish city-regions.

Housing

Housing conditions can have a strong impact on people's well-being. Housing satisfies several needs that go beyond having a roof over one's head. The house is also the place to rest, to provide security and protection, privacy, as well as the necessary space to have a family. With respect to other locations, cities are characterised by high residential density and thus relative scarcity of space. This implies also lower levels of affordability of housing and less space per capita, on average. Among the five Danish cities, the highest number of square metres per capita was observed in Aalborg in 2016.

Regarding housing affordability, Denmark appears to be more expensive than the OECD average. Housing cost plays a central role in families' budgets, and it is the main item of expenditure for households when taking into account rent, gas, electricity, water, furniture or repairs. Danish households spend on average 24% of their adjusted gross disposable income for their property, significantly more than the OECD average (18%). The Capital Region is the place where households spend the highest share of their income for housing (35%) (OECD, 2016b). As in other OECD countries, Denmark experienced a housing boom during the early 2000s, which was particularly strong in the city-region of Copenhagen, while much more moderate elsewhere (Figure 2.8). Housing prices increased sharply and then dropped after 2006, though in most urban locations prices are currently growing again. The housing boom and bust contributed to reduce the affordability of housing in Denmark, misallocate resources in the economy and amplify the effects of the economic crisis (OECD, 2016a).

Figure 2.8. **Inflation adjusted property prices in Danish cities**

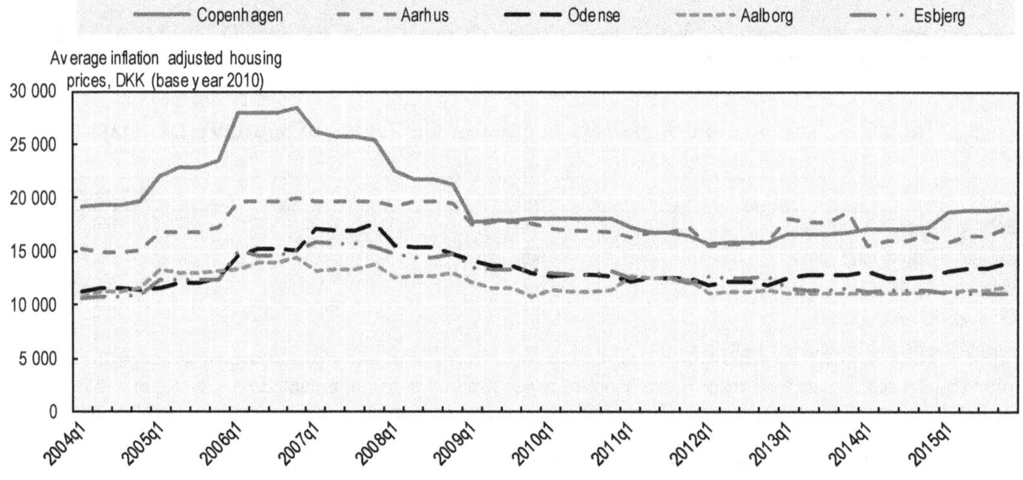

Note: Boundaries of city-regions are approximated to the closest municipal boundaries.

Source: Based on data from the Association of Danish Mortgage Banks.

Volatility in housing prices might have been amplified by property taxes, which are fixed in nominal terms and thus they are relatively cheaper for more expensive housing. The strict regulation of the rental market – the rent of dwellings built before 1991 are not freely determined – and the significant fiscal deductibility of mortgage interest rates in recent years were other elements contributing to the housing boom in the early 2000s (OECD, 2016a).

To ensure that the housing needs of citizens are met despite high residential property prices, Denmark has a relatively generous social housing sector. Around 22% of the dwelling rents are subsidised and determined at a level that covers only the operational costs (Ministry Housing, Urban and Rural Affairs, 2014), though long waiting lists exist. Another 20% of the housing stock is for private rent, but rents are freely determined only for dwellings built after 1991, which represent only around a fifth of the private rental market.

The composition of housing by tenure changes across city-regions and with respect to non-urban Denmark. On the whole, city-regions have higher proportions of dwellings occupied by tenants than by owners. Such a share includes both people who benefit from social housing subsidies and those who privately rent their home. The largest differences are not observed across city-regions, but inside them and between core cities and commuting zones (Figure 2.9). Such differences range from 31.2 pp in Aarhus to 16.5 pp in Esbjerg in 2016. In all city-regions and also in non-urban Denmark, the share of tenant occupied dwellings has been increasing since 2010.

Figure 2.9. **Proportion of tenant occupied housing in Danish cities**

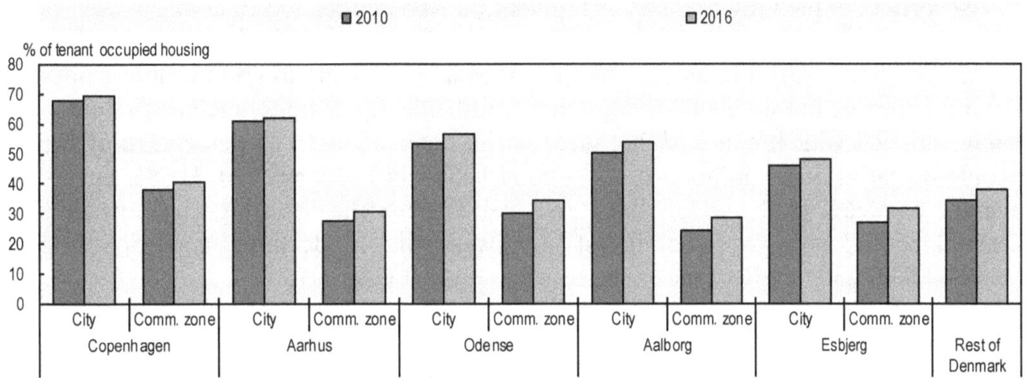

Note: Boundaries of city-regions are approximated to the closest municipal boundaries.

Source: Based on data from Statistics Denmark.

The affordability of housing is not the only important factor determining overall housing outcomes. The characteristics of dwellings and their basic equipment are crucial elements to be accounted for. Overcrowded housing, for example, can strongly affect people's quality of life by reducing physical and mental health and deteriorating social relations and personal development. In this context, Danish people benefit from high housing standards compared with other developed countries. Dwellings are generally of high quality, they host on average 2 persons in 55 square meters per occupant (Ministry of Housing, Urban and Rural Affairs, 2014). The OECD *Regional Well-being Database* provides the number of rooms per capita as the only comparable indicator for housing outcomes across all OECD regions. On average, in the OECD, people have 1.7 rooms per capita, while Danes have 1.8 rooms per capita. Focusing further on the availability of housing space and considering the square meters per capita, it is possible to distinguish the different dwelling space available to people living in the core and in the commuting zone in the cities of the Region of Southern Denmark. Overall, Figure 2.10 shows a similar pattern between Esbjerg and Odense. As expected, people living in the core have, on average, less space than those living in the commuting zone, though such difference is never higher than 10 m^2.

Figure 2.10. **Square meters per capita in cores and commuting zones of cities in the Region of Southern Denmark, 2015**

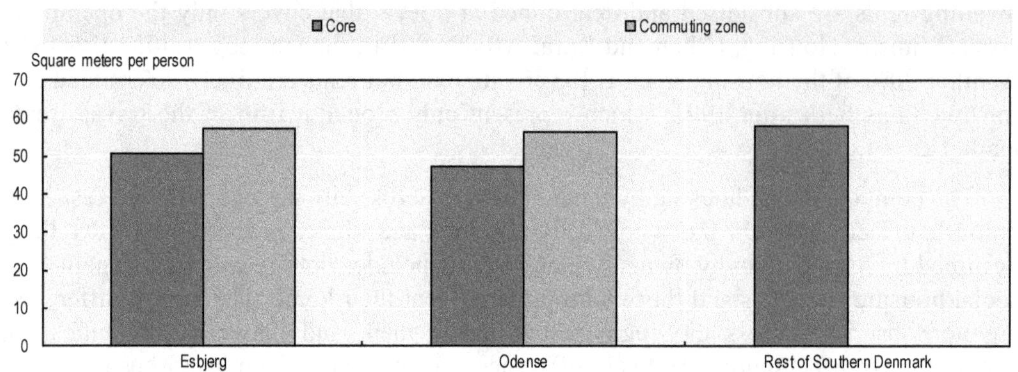

Source: Based on data provided by the Region of Southern Denmark.

Health

According to the OECD Better Life Index,[6] a web application to compare well-being across OECD countries, health is among the three dimensions of life that users value the most, along with work-life balance and life satisfaction. Being in good health is not only important per se, but it helps develop other well-being dimensions, such as finding a job, being satisfied with life and having good social connections. The percentage of Danish people declaring to be in good or very good health in 2013 reached 71.7%, against an average of 68.6% in the OECD. However, self-reported health is significantly different across income groups, with the highest and lowest quintiles declaring good or very good health in 83% and 66.5% of the cases, respectively (OECD, 2015b).

One of the headline indicators of health outcomes in the OECD Well-being Framework is life expectancy. At birth, Danish people are expected to live 80.4 years on average, which is in line with the OECD average. Again, there are differences across space. First, people living in one of the five Danish city-regions have a higher life expectancy than people living elsewhere, with such difference being around half a year.[7] Second, by looking within city-regions, it emerges that life expectancy is always (slightly) higher in the commuting zone than in the city-core, though Esbjerg is an exception. The city-region of Copenhagen shows large internal variation across municipalities in terms of life expectancy, with three municipalities (Lyngby-Taarbæk, Allerød and Rudersdal) showing the highest life expectancy among all Danish municipalities (around 82.4 years). At the same time, people living in the municipality of Copenhagen have the second lowest life expectancy (80 years) in Denmark, after Lolland (76.9 years) (Figure 2.11). In the period between the early 2000s (2000-04) and the first half of the 2010s (2011-15) life expectancy increased in all municipalities by, on average, almost three years. The largest increase – of around four years – is observed in the commuting zone of the city-region of Copenhagen, in the municipality of Egedal.

Overall, life expectancy in a municipality (both in levels and in terms of change since the early 2000s) is strongly and positively correlated with the median income and with the population size of the municipality (Figure 2.12). These correlations remain robust even when controlling for inequality, population growth, levels of education, risk of poverty and whether the municipality is located in the city-region or outside of it (see Annex 2.A2 for regression results). The correlation between life expectancy and median

Figure 2.11. **Life expectancy at birth in Danish municipalities by city-region**

Five-year averages (2011:15)

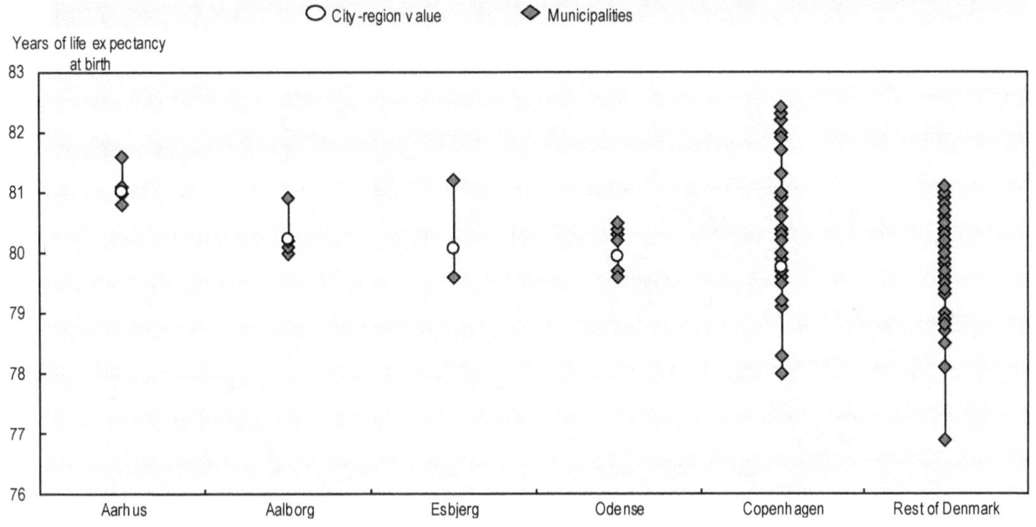

Note: Boundaries of city-regions are approximated to the closest municipal boundaries. Markers represent municipalities.

Source: Authors' elaborations based on data from Statistics Denmark.

income confirms the findings mentioned above regarding the perceived health status across income groups. It also suggests that the increase of income in the median household might also improve life expectancy, though no causal relationship can be claimed. On the other hand, gains in life expectancy are not correlated with a reduction of inequality or poverty rates, while recent analyses on US counties documented a negative though declining correlation between poverty rates and mortality rates of various population age groups (Currie and Schwandt, 2016).

Many important indicators of health outcomes other than life expectancy can be relevant to measure people's well-being. The obesity rate represents another important concern for policy makers, also because it is connected to other long-term health problems (diabetes, cardiovascular diseases, etc.) and potentially higher healthcare costs. While in Denmark obesity is relatively low compared with the OECD average, it increased from 9.5% in 2000 to 13.4 in 2010. Obesity is an example of an outcome that should be addressed by accounting for policy complementarities, since it is particularly sensitive to several other well-being dimensions, from income to accessibility to services. Child care services, for example, which are usually provided at the local level, can be important targets to address the obesity of children. Neelon et al. (2014) found that child care in the first year of life in Denmark was associated with higher weight at 12 months. Søren and Jo (2010) found that the prevalence of obese school children in Denmark was significantly higher in municipalities with low socio-economic status. In addition, parental child care has been found to have positive effects on children's behaviour. Research by Bonke and Greve (2012) found evidence that a one-hour increase in parental child care reduces the time children spent watching TV or on computer games by 20 minutes.

Figure 2.12. **Median income and life expectancy, Denmark**

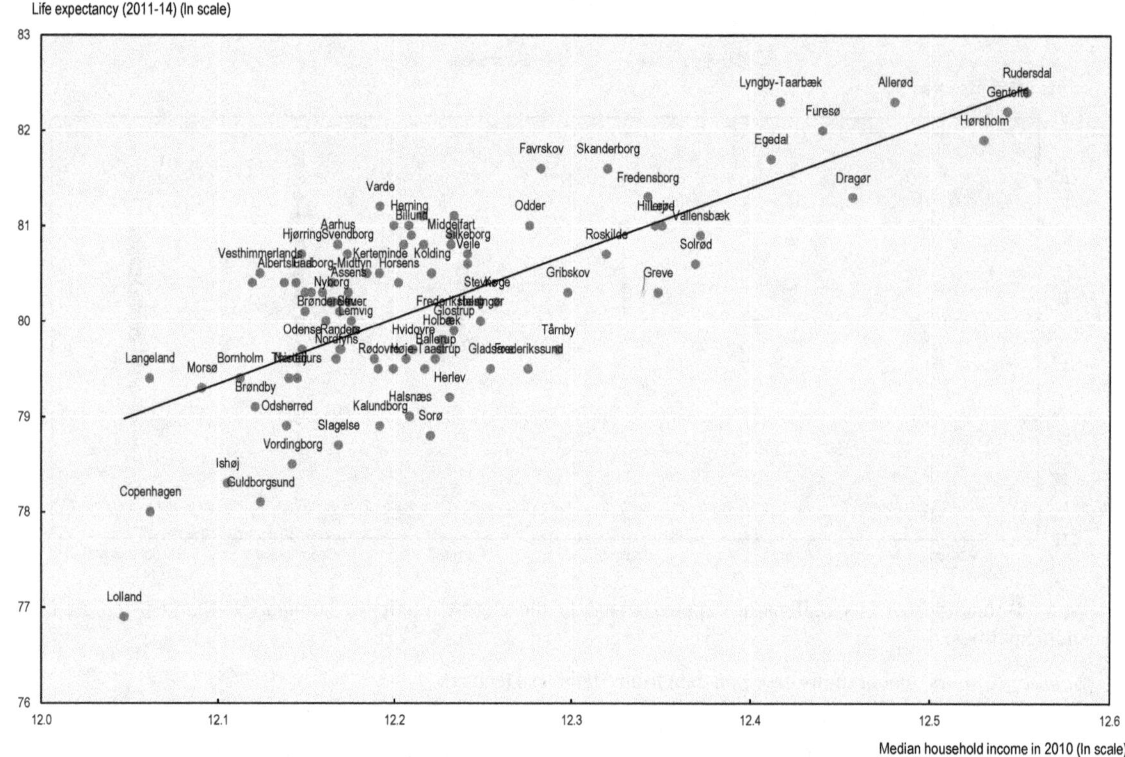

Source: Elaborations from Statistics Denmark.

The Danish Health and Medicines Authority (DHMA) is the most important health authority in Denmark. It develops quality standards, guidelines and works for health promotion, prevention and treatment. The DHMA also advises regional and local authorities and provides them with high-level targets and standards to be met, though regions and municipalities maintain some freedom in the organisation of healthcare. Significant variation has been observed in how quality assurance is organised across the different municipalities (OECD, 2013a). Greater coherence across initiatives and across levels of government would help exploit the strengths of Denmark's decentralised governance system.

Primary care is an important domain of health, especially in light of the increasing number of people living with multiple chronic conditions who need continued care provided in the community (OECD, 2013a). Among the indicators collected by the OECD on the (inverse) quality of primary care are the avoidable hospital admissions for long-term conditions, such as asthma and diabetes, which should be managed in many cases without recourse to hospitalisation. The age-sex standardised admission rate for diabetes improved by 5% between 2008 and 2013 (OECD, 2015c). The hospitalisation rate for diabetes shows a significant spatial variation across and within Danish city-regions, with Odense having the lowest rate (47.4), while Copenhagen had the highest one (75.4) in 2014.[8] Looking at the total number of hospital admissions, the latter disparities are confirmed among the city-regions, with Copenhagen having the highest rate and a gap of 7 000 hospitals admissions per 100 000 inhabitants compared to Aarhus. It appears, however, that no specific pattern seems to drive a core-commuting zone difference (Figure 2.13).

Figure 2.13. **Number of hospital admissions per 100 000 inhabitants in the cores and commuting zones of Danish cities, 2015**

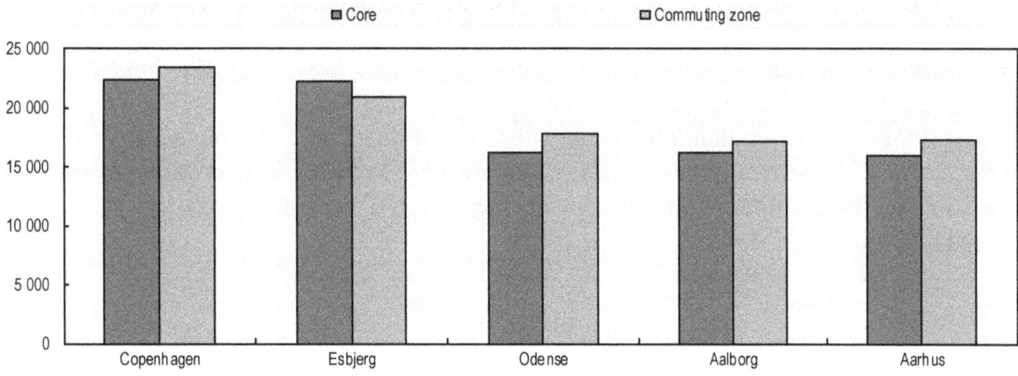

Source: Based on data provided by the Region of Southern Denmark.

Environment

Among the various well-being dimensions, environmental quality is one of those which changes the most across space. The quality of environment is, in fact, strictly related to the place considered and is sensitive to the intensity of human activities and economic processes. Exposure to air pollution, for instance, varies greatly depending on whether people live in more urban or rural locations. The OECD has developed a method to provide comparable measures of air pollution at different spatial scales across and within countries. Such a method combines satellite data with other geographic information, such as the population at the grid level, to measure the average exposure of the population in each city to the concentration of fine particles in the air ($PM_{2.5}$) (Brezzi and Sanchez-Serra, 2014; 2016). Based on this measure, for 53% of the OECD population in metropolitan areas, levels of air pollution were higher than the World Health Organization's recommended maximum of 10 $\mu g/m^3$ in 2013. Across the Danish city-regions, the average exposure to air pollution varied between 12.53 $\mu g/m^3$ on average in Copenhagen to 5.9 $\mu g/m^3$ in Aalborg in 2013.

Environmental outcomes are usually measured with objective indicators, such as air quality or, among others, green areas, water quality and biodiversity. However, identifying the specific natural places people think are attractive is challenging if one derives information only from the observable characteristics of land uses. Subjective assessments of environmental quality are seldom available, especially at the local level, though they are relevant to understand the extent to which the features of the environment where people live actually affects their levels of well-being. Natural amenities can lead to higher prices of nearby houses, they attract interregional migration flows and they increase individuals' life satisfaction (Bertram and Rehdanz, 2015; MacKerron and Mourato, 2013; Waltert and Schläpfer, 2010). Some studies have integrated objective and subjective information at the local level to analyse how natural amenities can affect people's well-being. One of those studies was carried out for Denmark, Germany and the Netherlands through an online survey called the Hotspot Monitor[9] (HSM) (Box 2.1) (Sijtsma et al., 2012; Daams and Veneri, 2016).

The HSM survey allows information of the exact location of attractive nature spots to be extracted from the respondents' answers. In turn, such "subjective" information is matched with the geographical boundaries of OECD city-regions (functional urban areas), in order to compute city-level indicators of perceived environmental quality. Compared to indicators based on land-use information, the HSM allows the identification of indicators to be based on people's preferences, grasping the heterogeneity of well-being potential among types of locations that would otherwise be considered homogeneous. A straightforward indicator based on the HSM measures how near the inhabitants of different cities live to highly attractive nature (Daams and Veneri, 2016). Such a measure captures, for each city-region, the average distance of its inhabitants' residential locations to the nearest high-amenity nature. By looking at this indicator it is possible to rank all cities in the three countries considered on the basis of their higher or lower level of natural amenities.

Box 2.1. **Measuring environmental quality through subjective indicators: The Hotspot Monitor Initiative**

The Hotspot Monitor (HSM) is an online survey tool that measures people's appreciation for natural areas. It was produced by a team of scholars co-ordinated by the University of Groningen in the Netherlands and builds on the widely used Google Maps tool. The central question for respondents in the HSM survey is: Which places do you find very attractive, valuable or important, and why? The only condition required of places to be considered in the survey is that they should be green and/or include water or nature. Based on these questions, the HSM survey measures each respondent's perception of the natural space's amenity value on a local scale (2 kilometres from the respondent's home), regional scale (20 kilometres from home), national and international scale. For each scale, the HSM survey respondents are asked to mark a single natural space they perceive as highly valuable.

The survey output includes point-location xy co-ordinates of the markers that respondents have placed to pinpoint natural areas (on both land and water), as well as the xy co-ordinates of their (approximate) living location. On the basis of the location markers for the respondent, clusters of natural amenities are identified. A cluster is a natural area in which HSM markers are more concentrated than would be expected if these were evenly distributed across space. Clusters of natural amenities with national relevance are identified in three European countries: Denmark, Germany and the Netherlands. Clusters are calculated per country, using only national HSM markers located in the observed country and cited by respondents of that country.

Source: Sijtsma, F.J. and M.N. Daams (2014), "How near are urban inhabitants to appreciate natural areas? An exploration of Hotspotmonitor based well-being indicators: Results for the Netherlands, Germany, and Denmark".

Looking at Danish city-regions, it appears that residents in Copenhagen and Aarhus have, on average, a higher physical proximity to the highly valued natural amenities, while people living in Odense have the lowest proximity (Figure 2.14). On average, Danish city-regions' inhabitants are 9.4 kilometres away from the closest highly valued natural amenity, while their German and Dutch counterparts are 9.9 and 5.7 kilometres away, on average. These results should be interpreted with caution, since they are based on individuals' perceptions, which in this case depend on people's knowledge about all natural amenities in a country. A possible bias can derive from the fact that people might tend to choose as most valued natural amenities those that are in proximity to the place where they live, since they may know less or be less attached to other natural amenities of the same country that are located further away from their place of residence.

Figure 2.14. **Population-weighted distance to highly valued natural amenities, Danish cities and some country averages, 2011**

Lower values mean physical proximity to high-valued natural amenities

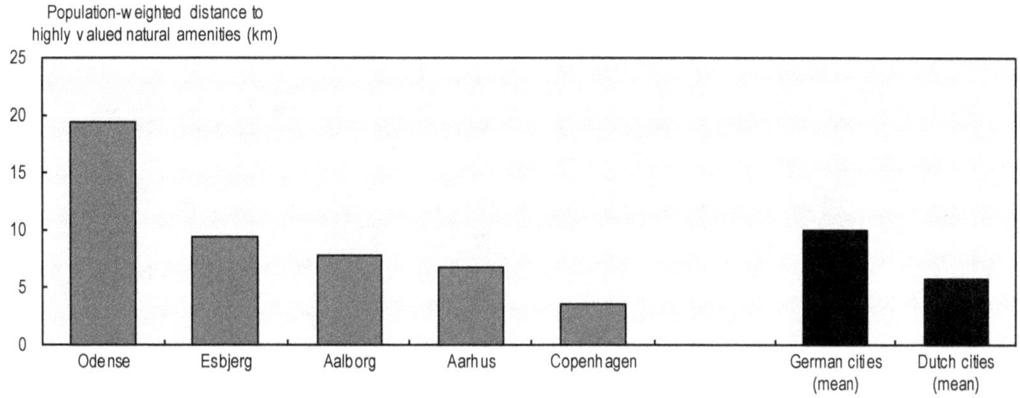

Source: Adapted from Daams, N.M. and P. Veneri (2016), "Living near to attractive nature? A well-being indicator for ranking Dutch, Danish and German functional urban areas", http://dx.doi.org/10.1007/s11205-016-1375-5.

Safety

Similar to environmental quality, personal security is strictly connected to the place where people live. Cities, regions and even neighbourhoods can be very different when assessed in terms of the incidence of crime. Besides its direct effect on the victims, crime affects people who are not directly victims but live in the same community. People's quality of life is dramatically affected by the occurrence of crime, since it increases the feeling of insecurity, while at the same time decreasing trust in others and in the institutions that are responsible for ensuring personal security. Overall, Denmark ranks towards the top of the OECD, being the country with the fifth lowest homicide rates and the fourth highest share of people (85.2%) who declare feeling safe when walking alone at night.[10] Denmark also ranks at the top in terms of security for children (OECD, 2015b).

Offences against people and property decreased in all Danish city-regions from 2007 to 2015, with the lowest decrease found in Copenhagen (-8% against more than -25% for all the other city-regions) (Figure 2.15). The offence rate reflects the total number of reported criminal offences per 100 000 inhabitants of a city-region. In 2015, Copenhagen had the highest offence rate of the five city-regions, at around 9 000 offenses, which supposes almost 1 offense per 10 inhabitants. The next highest city-region was Aarhus, at 7 000 offenses. The Odense city-region followed with a rate of 6 000 offences, close to the offence rate of the rest of the country (5 500 offences per 100 000 inhabitants).

Offences against property tend to concentrate in cities and the extent to which these crimes are reported increases with GDP per capita in Denmark, as in other OECD countries (OECD/IMCO, 2013). Reported criminal offences cover sexual offences, crimes of violence, offences against property and other offences. The share of offences against property always exceeds 90% (almost 95% for Copenhagen) of the total reported criminal offences, except for the city-region of Esbjerg. Sexual offences and violent crimes account for respectively approximately 1% and 5% of the total number of reported offences.

Figure 2.15. **Reported criminal offence rate in Danish cities**

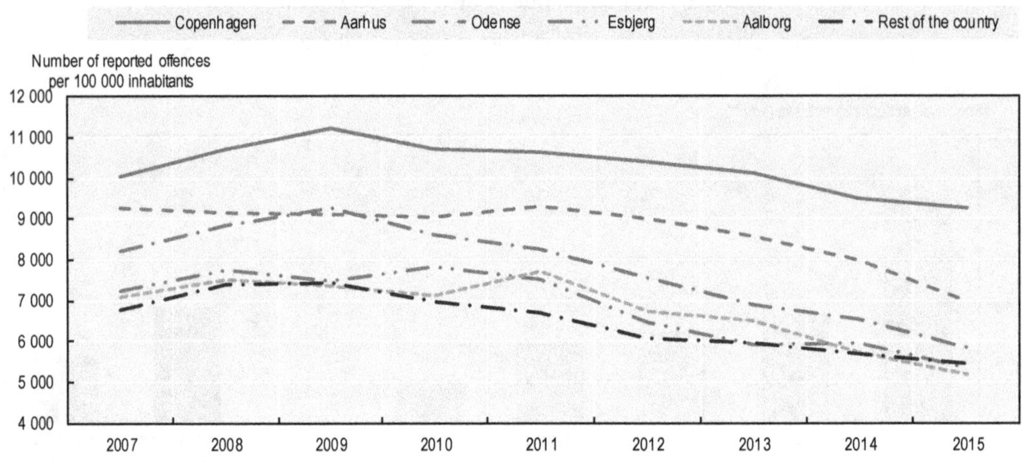

Note: Boundaries of city-regions are approximated to the closest municipal boundaries.

Source: Based on data from Statistics Denmark.

Overall, crime is an urban issue. All Danish city-regions have a homicide rate higher than that of the country except Esbjerg. Aalborg and Aarhus witness more than 1 homicide per 100 000 inhabitants, at 1.6 and 1.2 respectively. However, if we consider the country without the city-regions, the rate falls to 0.6. The homicide rate (the number of murders per 100 000 inhabitants) is a reliable measure of a city's safety level because, unlike other crimes, murders are usually always reported to the police. According to the latest municipal aggregated data, Denmark's homicide rate is 0.8, one of the lowest rates in the OECD, where the average homicide rate is 4.0.

Looking at violent crime, results reinforce previous findings that crime is higher in cities – especially in the core of cities – than elsewhere. The Danish city-region's cores typically experience more violent crimes per capita than their respective commuting zones (Figure 2.16). The case of the Copenhagen city-region is especially prominent, with almost twice the number of violent crimes committed in its core than in its commuting zone.

Figure 2.16. **Violent crime rate in the Danish cities cores and commuting zones, 2015**

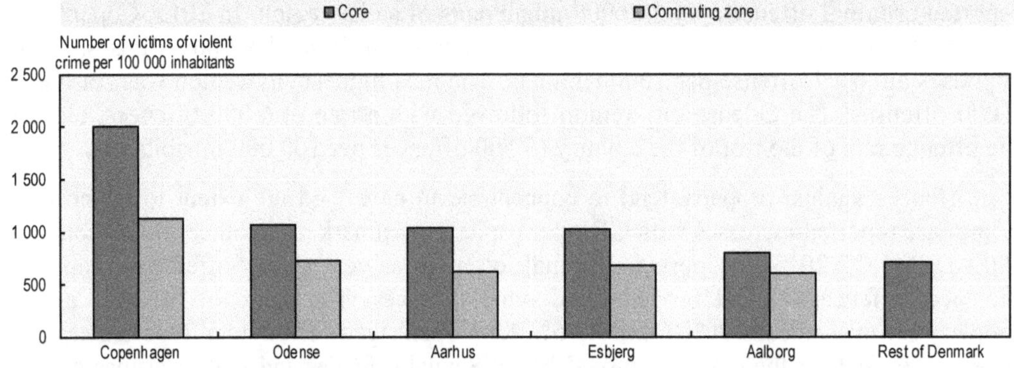

Source: Based on data provided by the Region of Southern Denmark.

Community (social relations)

Social relationships are a crucial source of well-being. They represent the most important resource to rely on when a person needs support and constitute an antidote to loneliness and unhappiness. More specifically, several empirical works have demonstrated that life satisfaction is significantly correlated with measures of social connections (Helliwell et al., 2010). In the later stages of life, both the size of individuals' social network and the frequency of contacts are associated with higher long-lasting life satisfaction. On the other hand, being isolated can make it more difficult to find a job and maintain good health. Social support can be provided by different people who are close to an individual, whether a partner, a family member, a friend or a colleague. The type of support provided by social connection can also be very different and include emotional, financial and practical support (e.g. caring for dependents, work-related support, etc.). The OECD Well-being Framework identifies a general measure of social connection, which is the share of people declaring having someone to rely on in case of need. This indicator is usually available through surveys, which are not always easily comparable across countries (Scrivens and Smith, 2013).

Overall, Denmark fares very well in terms of social connection, with 95% of people reporting having someone to rely on in case of need. The share was about 85% for the OECD (OECD, 2015b). On average, people living in city-regions seem to benefit from relatively higher social support than non-urban dwellers. This evidence is provided from the results of the Danish National Health Profile 2013, a survey where more than 160 000 Danes over the age of 16 were asked about health, morbidity and well-being issues. The two city-regions in the Northern part of the country – Aarhus and Aalborg – have the lowest share of people declaring not having anyone to talk to in case of need (Figure 2.17), followed by Copenhagen and then by the two city-regions of the Region of Southern Denmark, Esbjerg and Odense. Outside the territory covered by city-regions, a high variability in the lack of social support can be observed. The latter ranges from 8% in Lolland to only 2.5% in the municipality of Samsø, in the Central Region of Denmark.

Figure 2.17. **Lack of social support in Danish municipalities by city-region, 2013**

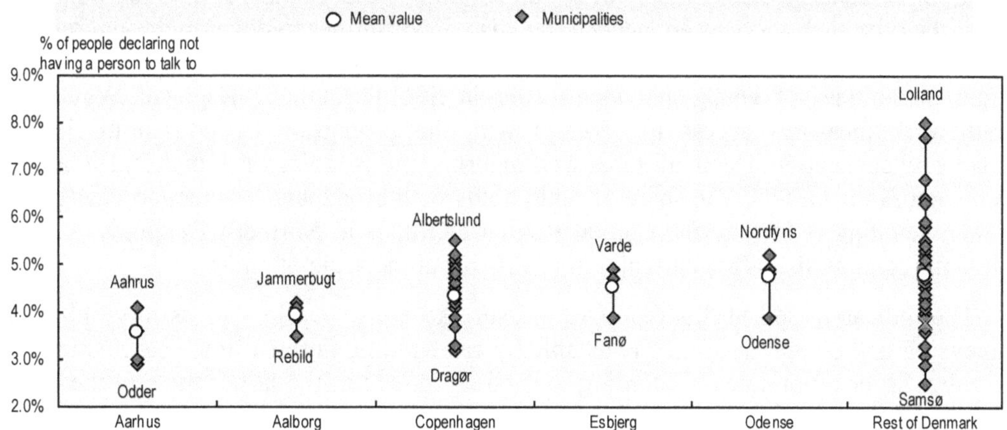

Source: Danish Health Survey.

Another indicator of social connection from the Danish National Health Profile 2013 is the feeling of loneliness of Danish people. On average, 5.7% of Danes declared feeling alone even though they would prefer being together with others. This share does not vary much across city-regions, ranging from 5.3% (Aalborg) to 6.2% (Esbjerg) in 2013. No significant changes are observed between 2013 and the first wave of the same survey, which was conducted in 2010. Instead, the most striking fact is that, within city-regions, the feeling of loneliness perceived by people is significantly higher for those living in the core cities rather than for those living in the commuting zone. Such difference is likely to be due to a composition effect, given that the characteristics (age, status, etc.) of people living in the commuting zone are different from those living in the core cities.

Access to services

Access to services encompasses a broad range of issues that are important for people's life. Measures of access to services can be broken down into several types of indicators, depending on the type of service and on the concept of accessibility that are taken into consideration. Services can refer to many domains, such as health, education or transport, for example. Many of them are considered separately as well-being dimensions and described in this report. On the other hand, according to the OECD Regional Well-being Framework, there are at last three types of accessibility, namely physical, economic and institutional (OECD, 2014). Physical accessibility refers to the extent to which it is easy for people to get to the place where the service is provided. Economic accessibility refers instead to the extent to which a given service is affordable. Finally, a service can be considered as institutionally accessible if there are no institutional factors such as laws, norms or social values that potentially or actually constrain such a service from being accessed by people. Physical accessibility is particularly relevant when well-being is assessed with a certain geographic detail, such as that of a region or of a city. According to where people live and to the extent to which the service is provided throughout space, physical access to a service can be very different across places. Not all cities in a country, for example, are connected in the same way to the national and international transport network and the same occurs within cities, where people living in the centre usually have greater access to a wider set of services in a shorter amount of time.

In many ways, access to services means access to opportunities. The extent to which people have access to a well-functioning health system, child and elderly care, or to good schooling or efficient public transport are all conditions that can affect not only quality of life at the time such services are needed, but also opportunities to develop throughout life. Going to a good school or having efficient healthcare, for example, is likely to affect the future possibilities of young individuals later in life. The OECD Regional Well-being Framework measures access to services with the proportion of households having broadband connection. Denmark fares well in terms of this indicator with the 11th highest value across the OECD. The share of households with broadband connection changes by region, standing at 89% in the Capital Region and 80% in Northern Denmark in 2014, while the same statistics are currently not available at the scale of cities.

The indicator used in this report to measure access to services in its more physical dimension is the number of jobs reachable by car within a defined time span, which can be either 30 or 60 minutes. According to such an indicator, the larger the city the larger the absolute number of jobs reachable within the time span considered. The relationship between the core and hinterlands depicts a different picture, depending on the city. When considering the shorter time of maximum commuting, the core emerges as more accessible than the commuting zone in all cities of Denmark (Figure 2.18). This is expected, since the higher employment density in the core allows a higher number of jobs to be accessible within a very short commuting time. It is also worth noting that such a higher accessibility in the core is particularly evident in Copenhagen. On the other hand, when the maximum commuting time is set to one hour, people living in the commuting zone have, on average, a higher accessibility to jobs in all cities, except in Odense. This suggests that living in the city core does not always guarantee a greater (physical) access to jobs, but instead depends on the commuting time one is willing to spend to go to work.

Figure 2.18. **Ratio between the mean number of full-time jobs reachable within 30 and 60 minutes, 2016**

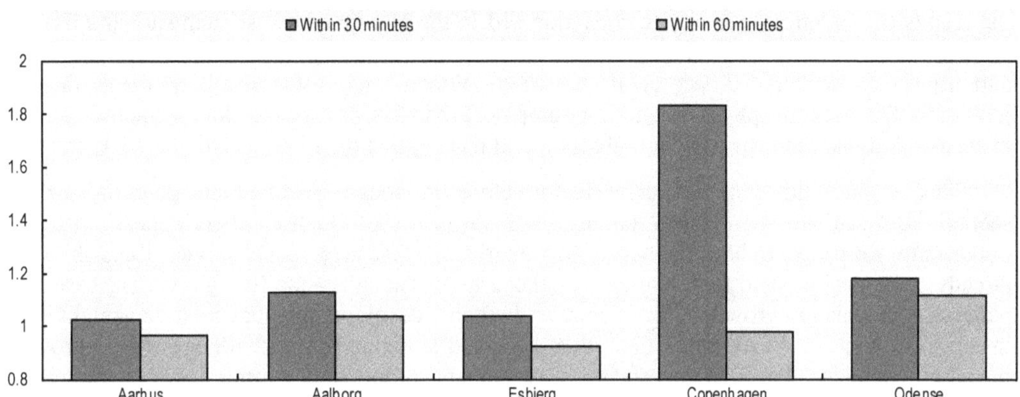

Note: Car traffic corresponds to rush-hour (7:30 am).

Source: Data provided by the Region of Southern Denmark.

Box 2.2. Measuring service accessibility as urban quality of life: Strategic research in the Region of Southern Denmark

Spatial analysis of service accessibility provides evidence to strategic planners and policy makers on how a city's distribution of people relates to key planning issues such well-being, urban attractiveness and even environmental performance. The geographic proximity to a service provides an opportunity for local residents, and can therefore be evaluated as a measure of well-being. This concerns both public services (such as health and education) that improve well-being, but also private services (such as grocery stores, restaurants, recreation centres, etc.) that people take advantage of in their everyday lives. In essence, the discussion concerns the assemblage of amenities located in the urban environment that allows people to meet their basic needs and improve the quality of their everyday lives.

While a comprehensive measurement of accessibility to either public or private services has not been completed for Denmark as a whole, the Region of Southern Denmark together with Nordregio has developed a new measurement approach using open source data. This has been applied in the area of Funen in Southern Denmark, as well as in three other Nordic city-regions (see Weber et al., 2016) for a complete overview of the methodological approach and Nordic findings). The hypothesis underpinning the work has been that: closer proximity to public and private services that local residents consume in their everyday lives offers a foundation for analysing well-functioning nodes in the urban form of a city-region.

The complete distribution of 20 public and private services have been mapped and measured. These have been categorised into five service groups (culinary, cultural and leisure, health, education, and commercial services) and further into ten service classes, forming a service accessibility index ranging from 0 to 10. A 20-minute walking distance on all roads and footpaths was chosen as the threshold to consider such services in proximity.

Box 2.2. **Measuring service accessibility as urban quality of life: Strategic research in the Region of Southern Denmark** (*continued*)

The first results presented for Funen show that the city-region exhibits a dispersed, polycentric pattern of service distribution, with a number of isolated settlement nodes surrounding the main regional centre of Odense having relatively strong service accessibility patterns. This specific type of core-periphery dynamic is particularly evident when comparing the results to the other three city-regions assessed in the Nordic analysis; each showing a more typical pattern of linear or corridor-like distribution patterns extending along main thoroughfares and transport corridors (Weber et al., 2016). In Funen, this is the result of many factors, including the lack of physical and topographical barriers to spatial development and the historical dominance of the agricultural sector and its resulting distributed settlement structure.

On one hand, this polycentric service structure provides a development potential for the second-order settlement areas surrounding the main centre of Odense. There appears to be an opportunity for people to have the best of both worlds in these areas: local service accessibility is already quite positive and there are also the benefits of "country-side living", which, based on patterns of population growth, age structure and income development, appears to be sought after in the local context. At the same time, this dispersed structure poses challenges for improving the significant dependence on the private car as a means of daily commuting. In short, there is no economically feasible way of further developing rail-based public transportation outside of the main city of Odense. This will necessitate the use of other technologies and innovative policies in order to promote more sustainable overall mobility on Funen.

Another component of the study has been to assess the above-mentioned core-periphery dynamic of dispersed settlements surrounding Odense in relation to ongoing demographic and socio-economic patterns. These results show, for example, that the strongest overall performance in terms of service accessibility combined with population development, household income, age structure and employment is exhibited in second-order towns, especially those located along the regional rail lines between multiple commuter catchments, as well as in the more traditional fringe areas around main urban settlements. At the same time, it is evident that many of the rural areas outside of these growth corridors will face issues of an ageing population and weakening service accessibility. This combination may pose severe limitations on the feasibility of market-based service provision in these rural areas, thus further worsening their already negative growth patterns.

The results of this type of analysis for Funen indicate a potential for second-order nodes outside the regional centre of Odense, particularly those with a good existing service base and, even more so, those located with access to the regional commuter rail services. In a more general perspective, the service accessibility results can have a range of uses for supporting the strategic planning of city-regions. Key examples include mobility infrastructure such as cycling networks, provision of public services such as education and healthcare. But perhaps most notably, when combined with spatial data on population distribution at the same scale, these results can be used to identify specific areas of service gaps and planning strategies to ameliorate them, as well as where strategic development potential exists around existing service clusters.

Source: Weber, R. et al. (2016), "A spatial analysis of city-regions: Urban form & service accessibility".

Civic engagement and governance

The engagement of people in public life and the right to express their own voice are essential outcomes in contemporary democracies. The engagement of people in the decision-making process also helps to make the government accountable and to strengthen trust in public institutions. Among the headline indicators of civic engagement and governance used in the OECD Well-being Framework is voter turnout, which is the percentage of eligible voters who cast a ballot in the national or local election. As several policies that directly affect people's lives are put into effect at the local level, this indicator can be particularly relevant to assess differences in trust in institutions and civic behaviour across cities.

Civic engagement in Denmark is high in international comparisons. Voter turnout is almost 86% of those registered in 2015, much higher than the OECD average, which was 68% according to the last available estimations (www.oecdbetterlifeindex.org). This indicator reflects a high civic engagement, also considering that Denmark is not among the countries where voting is compulsory (e.g. Australia, Belgium, Luxembourg and Turkey). Voter turnout has declined in two-thirds of OECD countries, especially since the start of the economic crisis in 2008 (OECD, 2015b) and the same trend characterised Denmark, where small decreases of voter turnout can be observed in all city-regions since 2007. Only seven municipalities in the entire country – all located in the commuting zones of city-regions or in non-urban locations – have shown a slight increase in political participation.[11]

The situation in Danish city-regions in terms of voter turnout is overall in line with that in the rest of the country (Figure 2.19). Differences across city-regions are not very large, since voter turnout ranged from 83.9% in Esbjerg to 86.4% in Aarhus in 2015. However, a significant difference is observed when looking within city-regions. In the commuting zones of Danish city-regions voter turnout is always significantly higher than in the core cities or in other locations of the country. As it was documented in the previous paragraphs, core cities concentrate a particularly high portion of unemployed, but also of highly educated people and tenant occupied housing. Tenants might be less engaged in the political process, especially at the local level, since they can move more easily instead of opting for staying and contributing to the progress of their community. There is also evidence that distance between the place of residence and the polling station in Danish municipalities has a significant negative impact on the probability to vote and the effect of such distance is sensitive to the availability of a car in the household (Bhatti, 2012).

Figure 2.19. **Voter turnout in Danish cities, 2015**

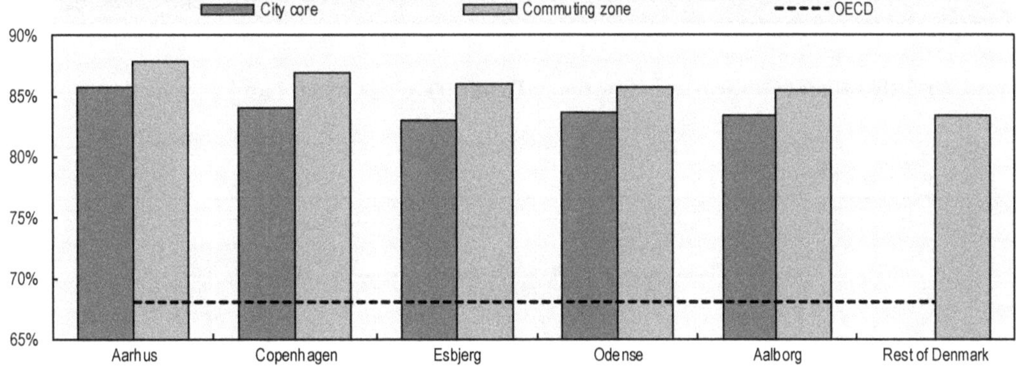

Source: Based on data from Statistics Denmark.

Life satisfaction

Life satisfaction is one of the most comprehensive indicators of subjective well-being. As for all the other subjective well-being measures, the idea is that the actual conditions experienced by people are as important as the way such conditions are perceived. People's judgement on how their own lives are going is as relevant as knowing about their objective situation and can effectively complement objective assessment of well-being and identify priorities for policy makers. Differently from objective measures, which are based on *a priori* hypotheses about the important dimensions in people's life, life satisfaction – and all subjective measures in general – reflect the actual preferences of people.

In most OECD countries statistical information on life satisfaction is collected in a consistent and comparable way through surveys, based on the OECD Guidelines on Measuring Subjective Well-being (OECD, 2013b). However, survey-based data are rarely available at the geography of cities, since the sample design allows producing information only at national or, at most, regional level. In the Region of Southern Denmark, the "Good Life" initiative carried out by the regional government makes it possible to assess people's well-being in all 22 municipalities. Such assessment is carried out through 25 perception-based indicators drawn from a survey with around 4 300 individuals interviewed 4 times a year (OECD, 2014). Once a year citizens are asked to assess their own level of well-being, both in terms of their overall life assessment and in terms of specific well-being dimensions (such as health, relations, etc.).

Danish people have high levels of life satisfaction. According to the OECD Better Life Index, Denmark has the highest level of life satisfaction among OECD countries, followed by Norway and Switzerland. The survey run by the Region of Southern Denmark assesses the life satisfaction of respondents on a scale from 0 to 100, with 100 as the maximum life satisfaction. Figure 2.20 shows that people living in the area outside city-regions have, on average, a slightly higher life satisfaction than their urban counterparts, though it is not known whether such a difference is statistically significant. The two city-regions of the Region of Southern Denmark show a different pattern of life satisfaction between the core city and the commuting zone. In Esbjerg, people in the commuting zone are relatively more satisfied than those living in the city core, while the opposite is true for Odense. This evidence is in line with the evidence provided above on jobs and education outcomes for the two city-regions. In terms of both dimensions (unemployment rate and educational attainment), living in the city-core rather than in the commuting zone is relatively better in Odense than in Esbjerg. Practically in all locations of Southern Denmark, life satisfaction increases with the levels of education and with the average household income.

Figure 2.20. **Life satisfaction scores in Southern Denmark cities by city and commuting zone, 2015**

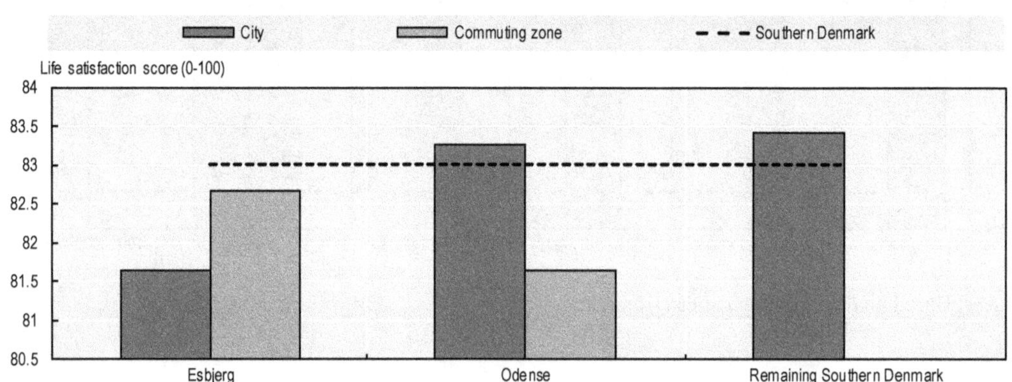

Source: Based on Southern Denmark's "Good Life" survey.

Improving the measurement of well-being in cities

This chapter has provided an assessment of well-being in the major Danish cities building on the OECD Regional Well-being Framework. With respect to regions, cities are more complex objects of investigation which bring about additional data challenges and specific issues to be analysed. As far as the statistical challenges are concerned, this chapter builds primarily on data available at the small area level, namely at the scale of municipalities, parishes[12] or small territorial grids. Information covering all aspects of well-being at this small geography is seldom available, even in the most developed countries. Administrative data provided by the Danish statistical offices and additional grid- level data provided by the Region of Southern Denmark made this work possible. Overall, a comprehensive assessment of well-being at the city level requires a further exploitation of administrative data. The scale of the territorial grid represents the benchmark in this respect, since it can be easily adapted to different geographies of interest.

Assessing well-being at the city level also requires considering specific issues which can be typically less important at a larger geography, such as at those of regions and countries. For example, the different patterns and trends of people's well-being across urban and rural locations is a natural issue to be investigated when working at the city scale. This report provides two perspectives to measure well-being across different types of territories according to their urban-rural continuum. First, it compares, when possible, well-being outcomes in the city-regions with those outside of them. In most cases, results highlighted higher well-being outcomes within city-regions than in the rest of the country. Second, it distinguishes the patterns and dynamics of well-being in the core of cities with those in the commuting zone. This type of perspective highlighted different living conditions in the two types of areas for many well-being dimensions, including income, jobs, civic engagement and safety, but also for the age structure of the population. Other issues of investigation that are specific to the city are those related to the spatial segregation of people within the different neighbourhoods. These issues are analysed in Chapter 3.

Notes

1. Household income is adjusted according to an equivalence scale in order to account for the different size of households. The equivalence scale is applied by dividing household income by the square root of the household size.
2. The OECD average refers to 18 OECD countries for which statistical information on income levels in metropolitan areas is available. These countries include Australia, Austria, Belgium, Canada, Chile, Denmark, Estonia, Finland, France, Hungary, Italy, Japan, Mexico, the Netherlands, Norway, Sweden, the United Kingdom and the United States.
3. See Boulant, Brezzi and Veneri (2016) for a detailed explanation of the method used to measure income inequality in cities.

4. The OECD average refers to the 282 metropolitan areas identified across 30 OECD countries by the methodology introduced in Chapter 1. Core and commuting zone in this case are approximated to the scale of the closest municipal boundaries.
5. Core and commuting zone in this case are approximated to the scale of the closest municipal boundaries.
6. www.oecdbetterlifeindex.org.
7. A t-test did not reject the hypothesis – at 99% confidence interval – that the mean life expectancy in municipalities belonging to city-regions is higher than mean life expectancy in the other municipalities. Such a difference has slightly increased since the early 2000s.
8. These figures are obtained from data at the municipal level, thus the value for cities is approximated to that of the area of the closest municipal boundaries.
9. http://hotspotmonitor.eu.
10. www.oecdbetterlifeindex.org.
11. The seven municipalities with increasing voter turnout are Assens, Billund, Favrskov, Frederikshavn, Rebild, Tønder and Vejen.
12. A parish in Denmark is an ecclesiastical community. Until the municipal reform of 1970, parishes were an administrative territorial unit. Even in the present day, the original parish boundaries still play a significant role, for example in determining community boundaries and school districts.

References

Bertram, C. and K. Rehdanz (2015), "The role of urban green space for human well-being", *Ecological Economics*, Vol. 120, pp. 139-152, http://dx.doi.org/10.1016/j.ecolecon.2015.10.013.

Bhatti, Y. (2012), "Distance and voting: Evidence from Danish municipalities", *Scandinavian Political Studies*, Vol. 35/2, pp. 141-158, http://dx.doi.org/10.1111/j.1467-9477.2011.00283.x.

Bonke, J. and J. Greve (2012), "Children's health-related life-styles: How parental child care affects them", *Review of Economics of the Household*, Vol. 10/4, pp. 557-572, http://dx.doi.org/10.1007/s11150-012-9157-6.

Bonke, J. and M. Schultz-Nielsen (2016), "Are working hour preferences satisfied?", *The Danish Journal of Economy*, Vol. 1, pp. 1-25, https://www.djoef-forlag.dk/sites/nt/files/2014/article/2014_1_4.pdf.

Boulant, J., M. Brezzi and P. Veneri (2016), "Income levels and inequality in metropolitan areas: A comparative approach in OECD countries", *OECD Regional Development Working Papers*, No. 2016/06, OECD Publishing, Paris, http://dx.doi.org/10.1787/5jlwj02zz4mr-en.

Brezzi, M. and D. Sanchez-Serra (2016), "Breathing the same air? Measuring pollution in regions and cities – updated results", United Nations Economic and Social Council, Economic Commission for Europe, Conference of European Statisticians, Sixty-fourth plenary session, Paris, 27-29 April 2016, https://www.unece.org/fileadmin/DAM/stats/documents/ece/ces/2016/mtg/CES_34-Breathing_the_same_air__OECD_.pdf.

Brezzi, M. and D. Sanchez-Serra (2014), "Breathing the same air? Measuring air pollution in cities and regions", *OECD Regional Development Working Papers*, No. 2014/11, OECD Publishing, Paris, http://dx.doi.org/10.1787/5jxrb7rkxf21-en.

Currie, J. and H. Schwandt (2016), "Mortality inequality: The good news from a county-level approach", *Journal of Economic Perspectives*, Vol. 30/2, pp. 29-52, https://www.aeaweb.org/articles?id=10.1257/jep.30.2.29.

Daams, N.M. and P. Veneri (2016), "Living near to attractive nature? A well-being indicator for ranking Dutch, Danish and German functional urban areas", *Social Indicator Research*, pp. 1-26, http://dx.doi.org/10.1007/s11205-016-1375-5.

Dahl, G.B. and L. Lochner (2012), "The impact of family income on child achievement: Evidence from the earned income tax credit", *American Economic Review*, Vol. 102/5, pp. 1 927-1 956.

Helliwell, J.F. et al. (2010), "International differences in the social context of well-being", in: Diener, E., J.F. Helliwell and D. Kahneman (eds.), *International Differences in Well-being*, Oxford University Press, New York.

MacKerron, G. and S. Mourato (2013), "Happiness is greater in natural environments", *Global Environmental Change*, Vol. 23/5, pp. 992-1 000, http://dx.doi.org/10.1016/j.gloenvcha.2013.03.010.

Ministry of Finance (2015), *Familiernes økonomi: fordeling, fattigdom og incitamenter 2015* (*Household Finances: Distribution, Poverty and Incentives 2015*), Copenhagen.

Ministry of Housing, Urban and Rural Affairs (2014), "Facts about Denmark", Danish Ministry of Housing, Urban and Rural Affairs.

Neelon, B. et al. (2014), "Early child care and obesity at 12 months of age in the Danish national birth cohort", *International Journal of Obesity*, Vol. 39/1, pp. 33-38, http://dx.doi.org/10.1038/ijo.2014.173.

OECD (2016a), *OECD Economic Surveys: Denmark 2016*, OECD Publishing, Paris, http://dx.doi.org/10.1787/eco_surveys-dnk-2016-en.

OECD (2016b), *OECD Regions at a Glance 2016*, OECD Publishing, Paris, http://dx.doi.org/10.1787/reg_glance-2016-en.

OECD (2016c), *Making Cities Work for All: Data and Actions for Inclusive Growth*, OECD Publishing, Paris, http://dx.doi.org/10.1787/9789264263260-en.

OECD (2016d), "Metropolitan areas", *OECD Metropolitan Database*, https://stats.oecd.org/Index.aspx?DataSetCode=CITIES.

OECD (2015a), *In It Together: Why Less Inequality Benefits All*, OECD Publishing, Paris, http://dx.doi.org/10.1787/9789264235120-en.

OECD (2015b), *How's Life? 2015: Measuring Well-being*, OECD Publishing, Paris, http://dx.doi.org/10.1787/how_life-2015-en.

OECD (2015c), *Health at a Glance 2015: OECD Indicators*, OECD Publishing, Paris, http://dx.doi.org/10.1787/health_glance-2015-en.

OECD (2015d), *OECD Population Database*, http://stats.oecd.org/Index.aspx?DatasetCode=POP_FIVE_HIST#.

OECD (2014), *How's Life in Your Region?: Measuring Regional and Local Well-being for Policy Making*, OECD Publishing, Paris, http://dx.doi.org/10.1787/9789264217416-en.

OECD (2013a), *OECD Reviews of Health Care Quality: Denmark 2013: Raising Standards*, OECD Publishing, Paris, http://dx.doi.org/10.1787/9789264191136-en.

OECD (2013b), *OECD Guidelines on Measuring Subjective Well-being*, OECD Publishing. http://dx.doi.org/10.1787/9789264191655-en.

OECD (2011), *Divided We Stand: Why Inequality Keeps Rising*, OECD Publishing, Paris, DOI: http://dx.doi.org/10.1787/9789264119536-en.

OECD/IMCO (2013), *Strengthening Evidence-based Policy Making on Security and Justice in Mexico*, OECD Publishing, Paris, http://dx.doi.org/10.1787/9789264190450-en.

Scrivens, K. and C. Smith (2013), "Four interpretations of social capital: An agenda for measurement", *OECD Statistics Working Papers*, No. 2013/06, OECD Publishing, Paris, http://dx.doi.org/10.1787/5jzbcx010wmt-en.

Sijtsma, F.J. and M.N. Daams (2014), "How near are urban inhabitants to appreciate natural areas? An exploration of Hotspotmonitor based well-being indicators: Results for the Netherlands, Germany, and Denmark", *URSI Research Report* 348, University of Groningen, Netherlands.

Sijtsma, F.J. et al. (2012), "Evaluation of landscape changes: Enriching the economist's toolbox with the Hotspotindex", in: Heijman, W. and C.M.J. v. d. Heide (eds.), *The Economic Value of Landscapes*, Routledge, London, pp. 136-164.

Søren, K. and C. Jo (2010), "The prevalence of overweight and obesity among Danish school children", *Obesity Reviews*, Vol. 11/7, pp. 489-491, http://dx.doi.org/10.1111/j.1467-789X.2010.00732.x.

Violante, G.L. (2008), "Skill-biased technical change", in: Durlauf, S.N. and L.E. Blume (eds.), *The New Palgrave Dictionary of Economics*, Second Edition, Palgrave Macmillan.

Waltert, F. and F. Schläpfer (2010), "Landscape amenities and local development: A review of migration, regional economic and hedonic pricing studies," *Ecological Economics*, Vol. 70/2, pp. 141-152, http://dx.doi.org/10.1016/j.ecolecon.2010.09.031.

Weber, R. et al. (2016), "A spatial analysis of city-regions: Urban form & service accessibility", *Nordregio Working Papers*, No. 2016:2, Nordic Centre for Spatial Development, Stockholm, www.nordregio.se/en/Publications/Publications-2016/A-Spatial-Analysis-of-City-Regions-Urban-Form--Service-Accessibility.

World Bank (2015), *A Measured Approach to Ending Poverty and Boosting Shared Prosperity: Concepts, Data, and the Twin Goals*, Policy Research Report, The World Bank, Washington, DC, http://dx.doi.org/10.1596/978-1-4648-0361-1.

Annex 2.A1.
Summary of data sources and scales

Table 2.A1.1 **Summary of data sources and scales**

Dimension	Indicator	Source	Scale at which data are provided	Year
Income	Equivalised household disposable income	Statistics Denmark	Municipality	2000-14
	Gini coefficient of household disposable income (inequality)	Statistics Denmark	Municipality	2014
	Household income group intervals	Region of Southern Denmark	Clustered 100 m grid (>100 households per cluster)	2013
Jobs	Unemployment rate	Region of Southern Denmark	Clustered 100 m grid (>100 households per cluster)	2003, 2013
	Labour force participation rate	Statistics Denmark	Municipality	2008-14
	Part-time employment	Statistics Denmark	Municipality	2008-14
	Youth unemployment rate	Region of Southern Denmark	Parishes	2013
Housing	Rooms per person	Statistics Denmark	Municipality	2016
	Square meters per person*	Region of Southern Denmark	100 m grid	2015
	Housing prices	Association of Danish Mortgage Banks	Municipality	2004-15
	Proportion of tenant occupied housing	Statistics Denmark	Municipality	2010, 2016
Access to services	Number of full-time jobs accessible by car within 30 and 60 minutes	Region of Southern Denmark	City-regions cores and commuting zones	2016
Safety	Homicide rate	Statistics Denmark	Municipality	2015
	Reported criminal offence rate	Statistics Denmark	Municipality	2007-15
	Number of victims of violent crime	Region of Southern Denmark	Clustered 100 m grid (>500 households per cluster)	2015
Education	Share of working-age population with a tertiary education	Statistics Denmark	Municipality	2006-15
	Share of working-age population with a tertiary education	Region of Southern Denmark	Clustered 100 m grid (>100 households per cluster)	2013
	Scores in Danish, English and mathematics*	Region of Southern Denmark	Point data at school level	2014-15
Environment	Air pollution: concentration of $PM_{2.5}$ in $\mu g/m^3$	Brezzi and Sanchez-Serra (2014; 2016)	Functional urban area	2013
	Distance to highly valued natural amenities	Daams and Veneri (2016)	Functional urban area	2011
Civic engagement	Voter turnout	Statistics Denmark	Municipality	2015
Health	Life expectancy at birth	Statistics Denmark	Municipality	2011, 2015
	Total hospital admissions	Region of Southern Denmark	Clustered 100 m grid (>500 households per cluster)	2015
	Uncontrolled hospital admissions for diabetes mellitus	Statistics Denmark	Municipality	2014

Table 2.A1.1. **Summary of data sources and scales** (*continued*)

Dimension	Indicator	Source	Scale at which data is provided	Year
Community (social connections)	Lack of social support	Danish Health Survey	Municipality	2013
	Feeling of loneliness*	Danish Health Survey	Municipality	2013
Life satisfaction	Satisfaction with life (on a scale from 0 to 100)*	Region of Southern Denmark's "Good Life" survey	City-regions cores and commuting zones	2015
Population	Number of persons and households	Region of Southern Denmark	100 m grid	2006, 2016

* Indicator only available for the cities in the Region of Southern Denmark (Esbjerg and Odense).

References

Brezzi, M. and D. Sanchez-Serra (2016), "Breathing the same air? Measuring pollution in regions and cities – updated results", United Nations Economic and Social Council, Economic Commission for Europe, Conference of European Statisticians, Sixty-fourth plenary session, Paris, 27-29 April 2016, https://www.unece.org/fileadmin/DAM/stats/documents/ece/ces/2016/mtg/CES_34-Breathing_the_same_air__OECD_.pdf.

Brezzi, M. and D. Sanchez-Serra (2014), "Breathing the same air? Measuring air pollution in cities and regions", *OECD Regional Development Working Papers*, No. 2014/11, OECD Publishing, Paris, http://dx.doi.org/10.1787/5jxrb7rkxf21-en.

Daams, N.M. and P. Veneri (2016), "Living near to attractive nature? A well-being indicator for ranking Dutch, Danish and German functional urban areas", *Social Indicator Research*, pp. 1-26, http://dx.doi.org/10.1007/s11205-016-1375-5.

Annex 2.A2.
Life expectancy and its correlates

This annex reports the results of regression analyses on life expectancy in Danish municipalities. In a first model, the mean levels of life expectancy in 2011-15 are regressed on a number of socio-economic characteristics. In a second model, the change in life expectancy between the early 2000s (mean 2000-04) and the early 2010s (mean 2011-15) has been used as the dependent variable. All variables used in the regressions are reported in Table 2.A2.1.

Table 2.A2.1. **Variables used in the regression analyses**

Variable	Description	Obs	Mean	Std. dev.	Min	Max
Dle	Growth in life expectancy	94	2.97	0.51	1.80	4.10
l_life11_15	Life expectancy in the early 2000s (ln)	94	4.38	0.01	4.34	4.41
l_life00_04	Life expectancy in the early 2010s (ln)	94	4.35	0.01	4.31	4.38
lpop2000	Resident population (ln)	98	10.62	0.77	7.73	13.12
ly5DC2000	Median household income (ln)	98	11.87	0.10	11.69	12.21
educ2006	Share of working-age population with a tertiary education	98	0.18	0.07	0.10	0.43
gini2000	Gini coefficient for household income	98	0.23	0.03	0.20	0.38
Dpop00_15	Growth of resident population between 2000 and 2015	98	0.03	0.08	-0.23	0.22
at_risk	Share of population at risk of poverty	98	0.04	0.01	0.02	0.11

Source: Statistics Denmark.

Results of the first and second model are presented in Tables 2.A2.2 and 2.A2.3, respectively. All coefficients were estimated using ordinary least squares (OLS) with robust standard errors.

Table 2.A2.2. **Regression results (ordinary least squares)**

Dependent variable: Levels of life expectancy in Danish municipalities, 2011-15 (mean)

Variable	mod1	mod2	mod3
pop	0.0012	-0.0002	0.0016
median income	0.0724***	0.0993***	0.0756***
educ	0.0374*	0.0074	0.0349
at_risk	-0.1333*		-0.1304*
gini		0.0157	
Dpop			-0.0062
constant	3.482***	3.162***	3.439***
N. observations	94	94	94
Adj. R2	0.592	0.581	0.588
City-region dummy	Yes	Yes	Yes

Legend: * p<0.1; ** p<0.05; *** p<0.01.

Table 2.A2.3. **Regression results (ordinary least squares)**

Dependent variable: Growth of life expectancy in Danish municipalities, 2000-15

Variable	mod4	mod5	mod6
l_life00_04	-22.05***	-21.16***	-21.48***
pop	0.3109***	0.2799**	0.2766**
median income	3.066**	3.496***	2.717*
educ	0.1939	1.2	0.3539
at_risk	-4.613		-4.571
gini		-3.715	
Dpop		0.2879	0.6665
constant	59.15*	50.9*	61.12*
N. observations	94	94	94
Adj. R2	0.226	0.2309	0.2213
City-region dummy	Yes	Yes	Yes

Legend: * $p<0.1$; ** $p<0.05$; *** $p<0.01$.

Results confirm that median income is always strongly correlated with both levels and growth of life expectancy in Danish municipalities. Levels of life expectancy are also significantly lower in municipalities with higher shares of people at risk of poverty. However, such municipalities do not show higher increases of life expectancy during the last decade. All else being equal, municipalities with a relatively larger population size, higher median income and lower initial life expectancy show a higher growth in life expectancy.

Chapter 3.

Well-being inside the city

This chapter provides an assessment of how well-being outcomes are distributed across different areas and neighbourhoods of Danish functional urban areas. It first describes what areas of cities have been growing the most in terms of population during the last decade. Subsequently, evidence on the patterns of spatial segregation by income and occupational status is provided and discussed, together with an analysis of the spatial concentration of youth unemployment.

Introduction

Policy makers at different levels of government have always had an interest in having information on well-being outcomes at a more detailed spatial level than the national and regional ones. Measuring income and employment status within small areas – including cities and neighbourhoods – is a crucial step to building basic information on living standards where people live as well as to investigating how population density changes over time. As cities grow, land values become increasingly differentiated due to increases in commuting costs and differences in the mix of public services and amenities. This, along with increasing income inequality, can foster a greater differentiation of residential neighbourhoods and a natural separation in space of different socio-economic groups.

This chapter assesses well-being outcomes within Danish cities, and identifies existing spatial patterns such as segregation of people by income, or clusters of unemployment and youth unemployment. The chapter starts with an analysis of population growth in the different areas of Danish cities, under the hypothesis that people chose their place of residence in order to maximise their well-being. Through a better knowledge of patterns of population growth, income and employment outcomes, policy makers can better identify the places where improvement is more needed and allocate public resources accordingly. The chapter also presents an assessment of the spatial segregation of households by income in the five major Danish cities and compares them with cities in other OECD countries. It also assesses concentrations of unemployment and youth unemployment across small areas (parishes) within Danish cities. Practically all of the results presented in this chapter are based on grid-level data provided by the Region of Southern Denmark.

Where do people reside within Danish cities?

The location decisions of individuals tend to reveal their current level of well-being and their own expectations. Looking at location choices is an alternative way to measure well-being across places compared to the use of surveys reporting subjective assessments of life or to objective outcome indicators in different dimensions (education, health, etc.). When a specific place shows persistent positive net population flows, it is likely that individuals expect their well-being to increase relatively more in the place of destination compared to their place of origin (Faggian, Olfert and Partridge, 2012). In other words, the idea is that people reveal the attractiveness of alternative locations by “voting with their feet” (Tiebout, 1956). In this perspective, patterns of population growth during the decade between 2006 and 2016 were observed across Danish parishes, the smallest administrative units at which population data are publicly available.

During the last decade Danish city-regions have increased their population at a higher pace than in the other parts of the country. Between 2006 and 2016, the average population growth rate of the parishes included within city-regions was 6.4%, while the mean growth in parishes outside city-regions was 0.06%. Looking within the city-regions, another fact that emerges in Denmark is that the average growth rate of parishes within the city cores is significantly higher than that in the parishes included in the commuting zones (10.2% and 3.9%, respectively). In other words, the population in Danish city-regions has been “centralising” or more spatially concentrating during the last decade. This pattern is consistent with the results of recent work analysing population growth patterns within OECD functional urban areas in 29 OECD countries (Veneri, 2015). According to that study, while in the majority of countries relatively higher increases in the commuting zone were documented rather than in the city-cores, in a small number of countries – including Denmark, Austria, Belgium, Luxembourg, the Netherlands and Sweden – the pattern of growth has been opposite, with higher population increases in the city cores, which are already the densest areas of their respective city-regions.

Population has grown unevenly within the city-regions and it was stronger in parishes which had a larger initial population size and that are closer to the main population centres. Figure 3.1 shows the rates of population growth in the different parishes of the city-region of Odense between 2006 and 2016. In the specific case of Odense, the largest increases in population occurred in the central and eastern part of the city-region. The factors associated with population growth in Danish parishes within the boundaries of city-regions were identified through a regression analysis (ordinary least squares method) carried out at the parish level, also to test whether there is a tendency toward a higher concentration of population in locations that are already central and denser. The cumulative growth rate of population in each parish was regressed on population density, the logarithm of resident population and a measure of physical distance of each parish to the most "central" and high-density parish in each city-region. Such central parishes are identified as the parishes with the largest population size located in the core of each city-region with, at the same time, a level of population density included in the top 10% of city-regions' parishes in 2006. Regression results are reported in Table 3.1.

Figure 3.1. **Population growth in the parishes of Odense's cities, 2006-16**

Source: Based on data provided by the Region of Southern Denmark.

Table 3.1. **Regression results on the population of parishes in Danish cities, 2006-16**

Ordinary least squares with robust standard errors

Variable	Mod1	Mod2
Population density (2006)	1.8e-06*	2.1e-06**
Distance from the main centre (ln)	-0.0117***	
Distance from the main centre		-0.063**
Square of distance from the main centre		0.0068**
Total population (ln)	0.0099***	0.0093***
Constant	-0.0171	0.0227
N. observations	763	768
Adj. R2	0.210	0.207
City-region/core-commuting zone controls	Yes	Yes

Source: Based on data from Statistics Denmark.

City centres attract a younger population. The age structure of the population reflects the positive dynamics of the cores in Danish city-regions. In all five city-regions, the proportion of the population over 65 years old is higher in the commuting zone than in the city cores. In Aarhus this difference is about 3 percentage points, with the core and the commuting zone having 14.7% and 17.7% of elderly people, respectively in 2016. This tendency has been increasing in recent years. In Copenhagen, for example, the share of elderly people in the city core has been almost stable since 2008 (+0.4 pp), while in the commuting zone there has been an increase of almost 5 percentage points in the same period. All Danish cities show similar patterns during the last years.

The spatial segregation of people by income

Cities are places where inequality manifests also in its more spatial dimension. When looking at what happens within a city-region, inequality often translates into various forms of spatial segregation (OECD, 2016). Spatial segregation is a situation where people sort within the space of a city-region in a way that generates an over-concentration in specific places of people who are similar with respect to certain socio-economic lines, such as income, race or socio-economic status. The most recent literature documents an increase in spatial segregation over the last couple of decades in most developed countries (Massey et al., 2009; Rothwell and Massey, 2010; Tammaru et al., 2016). Such an increase was particularly strong for income segregation, while at the same time, at least in the United States, racial segregation has been decreasing (Glaeser and Vigdor, 2012; Logan and Stults, 2011).

In order to measure income segregation, spatial ordinal entropy indexes were computed for 2013 using 1-hectar grid-level data on household income levels (Box 3.1).[1] Figure 3.2 shows the levels of segregation by income in all five Danish city-regions and in comparison with the average segregation for the metropolitan areas in four other OECD countries (Canada, France, the Netherlands and the United States). Danish city-regions are, on average, less segregated by income than those in Canada and the United States, while they show values similar to those of other European cities. There is also less variability across European cities, as standard deviation is low compared to that found across their North American counterparts (0.01 and 0.02, respectively).

Figure 3.2. **Levels of spatial segregation by income in Danish cities and some country averages**

Spatial Ordinal Entropy Index (within 1 kilometre radius); higher value means higher segregation

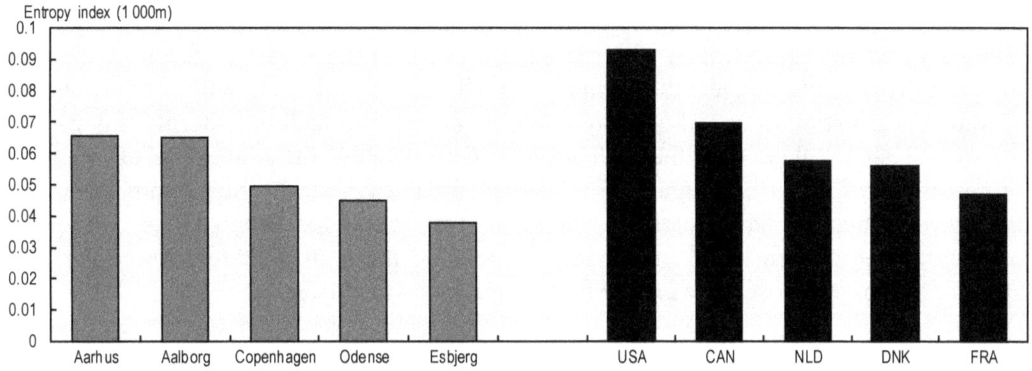

Notes: Data refer to 2014 for the United States; 2013 for Denmark; 2011 for Canada and France; 2009 for the Netherlands. Country averages (on the right) refer to the mean of all city-regions (functional urban areas with more than 500 000 inhabitants) in the respective countries. In the case of Denmark, country average covers all five city-regions.

Source: Authors' calculations based on national income data.

Spatial segregation is a natural urban phenomenon. People locate in different parts of a city according to their preferences and subject to their limited resources, so that the clustering of similar people does not necessarily represent a negative or positive outcome. There is extensive literature studying the consequences of spatial segregation and it is not easy to identify solid economic arguments to consider it as a possible ground for policy intervention.

The most affluent households often cluster because they want a more homogeneous environment and access to the best public services and schools. This in turn benefits the most affluent people further, though it also translates into further increasing inequality (Morrison, 2015). Living among similar people can even reduce conflict and give people a sense of safety. A certain level of segregation can also enhance social support through strong networks, which might also benefit the integration of migrants (if clustered).

One of the darker sides of segregation is the involuntary concentration of disadvantage, meaning the spatial concentration of poverty. People in the lowest tail of the income distribution do not really have much margin to choose their location within the city and they often end up living in places where public services are underprovided or of low quality and with a deteriorated social environment. When this is the case, people living or growing up in the poorest neighbourhoods might have permanent disadvantages in terms of socio-economic mobility, health and education (Chetty, Hendren and Katz, 2015; Van Ham et al., 2012). Highly segregated cities might also worsen the spatial mismatches between affordable housing for low-income households and the jobs they can find (McKenzie, 2016: 368). In addition, living in a deprived neighbourhood has been found to be persistent across generations and to be stronger for racial minorities than for other groups of people (Vartanian, Buck and Gleason, 2007; Sharkey, 2008; de Vuijst, van Ham and Kleinhans, 2015).

Spatial segregation can be of different types. In this respect, the type of spatial segregation by income of Danish city-regions is different from that in Canada, France or the United States. In principle, similar people tend to cluster in space, but such a tendency can be stronger for specific social groups. Evidence shows that in most cases the most affluent people are those who tend to concentrate the most in specific neighbourhoods, which are inaccessible to other groups. This is the case, for example, in the major city-regions in Canada, France and the United States (OECD, 2016). Despite their relatively low values, in Danish city-regions the poor are those who concentrate the most in space. This might suggest the formation of disadvantaged areas within cities and the spatial concentration of social housing could be among the factors fostering this pattern. Figure 3.3 shows that, with the exception of Copenhagen, the highest level of spatial segregation in Danish city-regions is observed for the people in the bottom tail of the income distribution. This pattern is similar to that found for Dutch cities, while it is opposite to the pattern found in Canada, France and the United States, where the most affluent groups are those showing the highest tendency to cluster.

Figure 3.3. **Spatial segregation by income groups**

Spatial ordinal entropy index (within 1 kilometre radius)

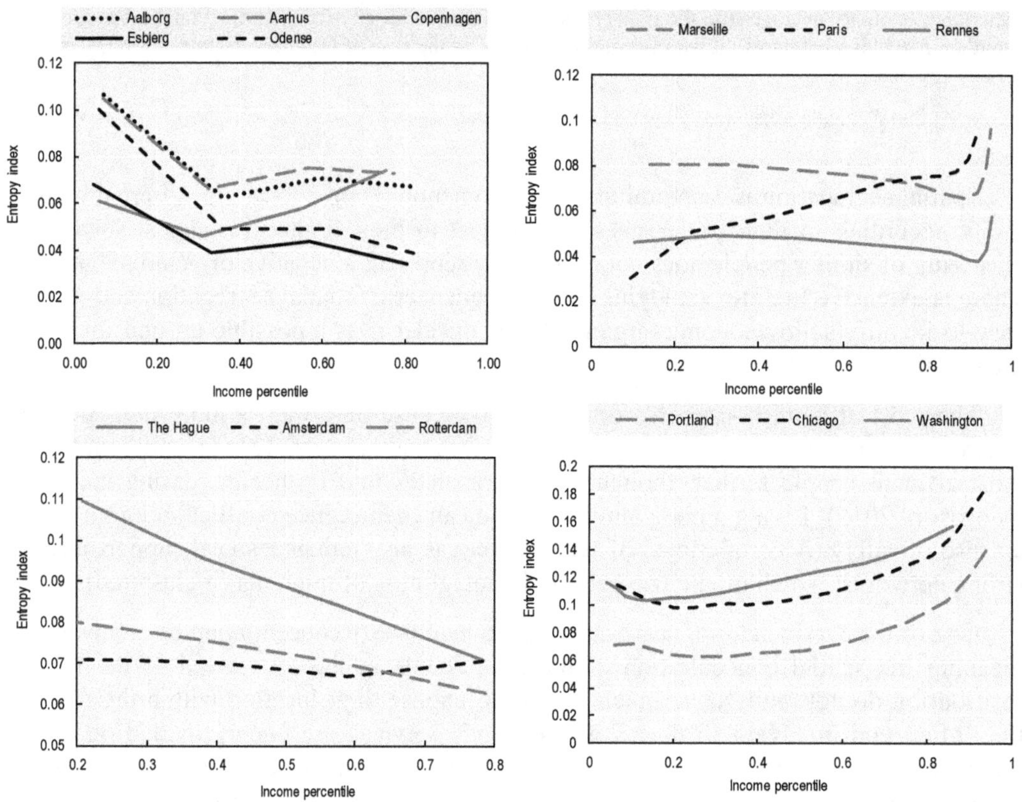

Note: Data refer to 2014 for the United States; 2013 for Denmark; 2011 for France; 2009 for the Netherlands.

Source: Based on OECD (2016), *Making Cities Work for All: Data and Actions for Inclusive Growth*, http://dx.doi.org/10.1787/9789264263260-en.

Box 3.1. How to measure segregation?

The term segregation refers to the physical separation of two or more groups into different neighborhoods. There are many ways to measure segregation. This box presents the ones used in this report.

Dissimilarity Index

The best known measure of segregation is the Dissimilarity Index. The Dissimilarity Index can only be applied to two groups at a time, an approach that reflects its application to questions of racial segregation. However, this index can also measure the relative separation of socio-economic groups across all neighbourhoods of a city. A socio-economic Dissimilarity Index of, for example, 40 (comparing poor and rich), would mean that 40% of poor people would need to move to another neighbourhood to make poor and rich people evenly distributed across all neighbourhoods. The Dissimilarity Index can be computed as follows:

$$D = \frac{1}{2}\sum_{i=1}^{n}\left(\frac{h_i}{H_T} - \frac{l_i}{L_T}\right) * 100$$

where n is the number of neighbourhoods; h_i is the number of members of one group (e.g. highest socio-economic group) in neighbourhood i; H_T is the total number of this group members in the city; l_i is the number of members in the other group (e.g. lowest socio-economic group) in neighborhood i; and L_T is the total number of this group members in the city.

Spatial Ordinal Entropy Index

The Spatial Ordinal Entropy Index can be computed using grid cells data to create local environments or neighbourhoods that are defined at different scales. For example, spatial entropy at a 1 000 m scale takes each grid cell and defines a 1 000 m area surrounding it as the neighbourhood. The Ordinal Entropy Index is the ratio between the proportion of the population from each income group in this neighbourhood to that in the city. Given the large number of cells that approximate a surface distribution, integrals are used for the calculations, which are as follows:

$$\tilde{\Lambda} = \int_{p \in R} \frac{t_p}{T} \cdot \frac{v - \tilde{v}_p}{v}$$

where T is the city population and t_p is the population of the neighbourhood, v and $\tilde{v}_p$ are the entropy for the city and the neighbourhood respectively and the latter is calculated as follows:

$$\tilde{v}_p = -\frac{1}{M-1}\sum_{m=1}^{M-1} \tilde{c}_{pm}\, log_2 \tilde{c}_{pm} + (1 - \tilde{c}_{pm}) log_2 (1 - \tilde{c}_{pm})$$

where M is the number of income groups and $\tilde{c}_{pm} = \sum_{k=1}^{m} \tilde{\pi}_{pk}$ is the cumulative income share in the neighbourhood p for each cell in the surface grid, with $\tilde{\pi}_{pk}$ being the share of the population in income group k. The same procedure is applied for each neighbourhood to obtain v.

The Spatial Ordinal Entropy Index as a measure of income segregation has several advantages. For instance, it allows considering several income groups instead of only two and it minimises the modifiable areal unit problem by eliminating borders and relying on the surface distribution of individuals.

Box 3.1. **How to measure segregation?** *(continued)*

Local Moran's Index

Although it is the least well-developed, another approach to measure segregation derives from the geographical notion of spatial autocorrelation. Spatial autocorrelation statistics depend on the definition of neighbourhoods' relationship selected prior to analysis. Considering that the entire neighbourhood is relevant when it is not too large, a method not letting too many isolated points as the k-neighbour approach is suitable, because it leaves no polygons without neighbours. It actually treats the nearest k block groups as neighbours.

To identify local patterns of spatial autocorrelation, one can use the locals Moran's *I*. Unlike the global Moran's *I*, which has the same value for the entire study area, the value of local Moran's *I* varies for each location because it is calculated in relation to its particular set of neighbours. Using this statistic, one can calculate separate estimates of segregation for each spatial unit of analysis.

Source: OECD (2016), *Making Cities Work for All: Data and Actions for Inclusive Growth*, http://dx.doi.org/10.1787/9789264263260-en.

Spatial inequalities in employment outcomes

Urban residents usually locate close to other people having similar characteristics, which in some cases might generate patterns of physical separation between groups of people in different neighbourhoods. In some cases, it can happen that this stratification is strong and regards the more disadvantaged people, with possible implications on individual outcomes, such as the probability of being employed. In other words, different characteristics of the place of residence can provide different levels of access to employment. In a process known as "spatial mismatch" (Kain, 1968), residing in places which are far and not well connected to job centres might have consequences in terms of wage levels and unemployment. Among the mechanisms driving the potential different outcomes are physical distance to jobs and/or the weakness of the transport and social network.

Unemployment rates can be very different in the neighbourhoods of Danish city-regions, as unemployed people do not seem to over-concentrate in space following a simple core-commuting zone pattern (Figure 3.4). In general, there are parishes with a particularly high concentration of unemployed in a scattered way throughout the city-region, though, with the exception of Esbjerg, unemployment rates are, on average, higher in the cores of the cities.

In order to assess more precisely the pattern of clustering of the population of Danish city-regions by their employment status, a Dissimilarity Index was computed and is shown in Table 3.2. The Dissimilarity Index is an index of segregation, ranging between 0 and 100, and measuring the percentage of one group of people (e.g. the unemployed) that would have to move across neighbourhoods to be distributed the same way as the second group (e.g. employed). A Dissimilarity Index of 0 indicates a situation in which both groups are distributed in the same proportions across all neighbourhoods, while an index close to 100 indicates a situation of maximum segregation, where the members of one group are located in completely different neighbourhoods than those of the second group (see Box 3.1).

Figure 3.4. **Unemployment rate of 25-64 year olds within the Danish cities, parish level, 2013**

Source: Elaboration with data provided by Southern Denmark region.

Figure 3.5. **Unemployment rate of 25-64 year olds within the Copenhagen city-region, parish level, 2013**

Source: Elaboration with data provided by Southern Denmark region.

Among the Danish city-regions, the highest level of segregation by employment status is observed in Esbjerg and in Copenhagen, with values of 32.1 and 28.9, respectively. These values might be compared with other European cities by considering the recent study of socio-economic segregation in European capital cities by Tammaru et al. (2016). However, any comparison should be interpreted with caution, since any measure of segregation might depend on the scale of the spatial unit of analysis (parishes in the Danish case). Given these caveats, note that in comparison, the city of Milan, Italy, had a Dissimilarity Index between unemployed and employed people of 26.7 in 2001 (Tammaru et al., 2016). Only one of the Danish city-regions – Odense – had a lower level of segregation, with Aarhus having a close value and the rest of the city-regions showing higher values.

Spatial segregation by employment status tends to be relatively higher in the city cores than in the commuting zones of Danish city-regions (Table 3.2). An exception is the city-region of Copenhagen. As in the other city-regions, in Copenhagen the unemployment rates in the core is relatively higher than those in the commuting zone. However, such higher unemployment is relatively evenly distributed spatially, which explains why the Dissimilarity Index is lower than in the commuting zone. During the late 1980s and early 1990s, the city underwent a long-term urban crisis which brought it close to bankruptcy and to problems including deindustrialisation, unemployment, an outdated housing market, and strong ethnic and income segregation (Andersen and Winther, 2010). It followed an urban upturn and, today, Copenhagen is a strong national centre for economic growth (Winther, 2007; Hansen and Winther, 2010). However, the core still has higher unemployment rates than other parts of the city-region (Figure 3.4).

Table 3.2. **Dissimilarity indexes for employment status within Danish cities**

Unemployed vs. total employed, grid-level data, 2013

	City region	Core	Commuting zone
Aalborg	27.8	26.5	27.0
Aarhus	27.3	26.0	26.0
Copenhagen	28.9	25.9	32.0
Esbjerg	32.1	31.2	27.7
Odense	26.5	31.1	22.4

Source: Elaboration with data provided by Southern Denmark region.

Job loss and unemployment depress the mental health of those affected with long-term scarring effects, especially in the case of youth unemployment. Indeed, youth unemployment might lead to several negative outcomes in terms of both material and mental well-being (Paul and Moser, 2009). The negative impact of unemployment on a young person's sense of well-being can be even stronger if concentrated in the same areas. Using local measures of spatial correlation (Moran's *I*), youth unemployment segregation at the parish level for the whole of Denmark is assessed. The values of local Moran's *I* vary for each parish because it is calculated in relation to its particular set of parish neighbours. Here, the four nearest parishes were chosen as the neighbouring criterion in order to form the possible area of concentration.

Denmark shows several places concentrating youth unemployment, which are mostly located outside the main cities or close to their external borders (Figure 3.6). The concentration of youth unemployment is assessed through a hotspot analysis at the parish level. A hotspot is a place where high values of youth unemployment cluster together. This situation corresponds to both positive and significant (p-value<0.05) local Moran's *I* along with a youth unemployment rate higher than the mean. The hotspots of youth unemployment for the whole of Denmark seem to concentrate in two main areas: first, the western and southern lands of Copenhagen and second, around but also inside the city-region of Aalborg (Figure 3.6).

Figure 3.6. **Hotspots of unemployment rate of 15-24 year olds within the Danish cities, parish level, 2013**

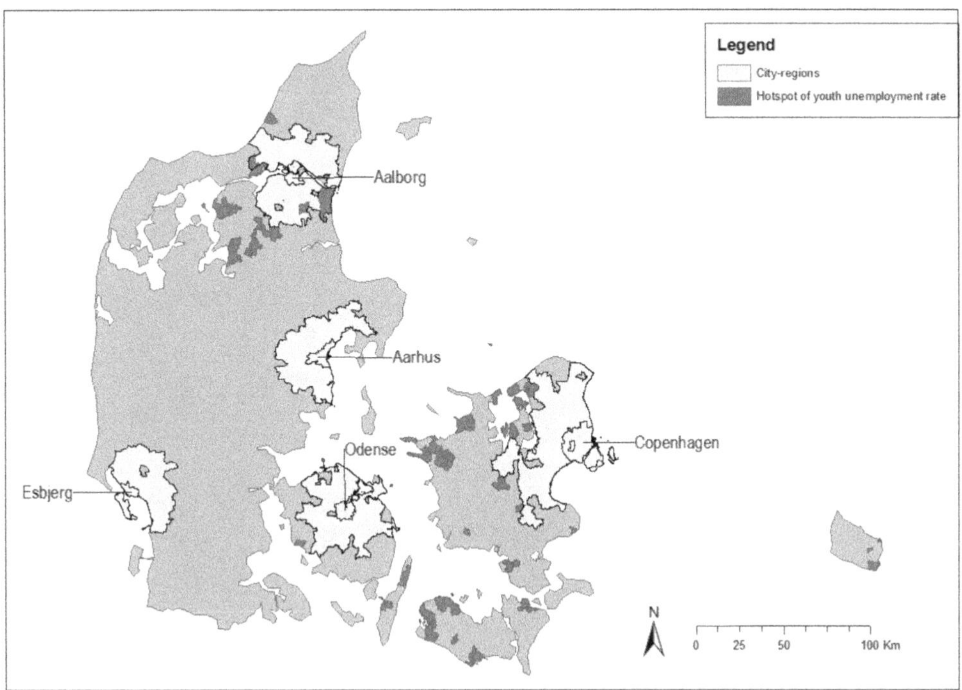

Source: Elaboration with data provided by Southern Denmark region.

Summary and data challenges

This chapter helps identify how Danish cities differ in terms of the extent to which advantages and disadvantages are distributed within their respective territory. First, the analysis on population growth reveals that population is concentrating in already large and dense places close to the main centres. The Odense city-region appears to be the one with the most uneven population growth within its area over the last decade. However, differences in well-being outcomes can also be observed in terms of income and jobs outcomes. Households with different incomes tend to concentrate in socially homogeneous neighbourhoods, and, differently from what happens in other OECD countries, low-income households are those which tend to segregate the most. The spatial segregation of people by employment status (employed vs. unemployed), on the other hand, is higher in the cores than in the commuting zones of Danish cities, with the exception of Copenhagen, where relatively high levels of unemployed can still be observed in the core. Clusters of youth unemployment are instead observed mainly outside the major Danish cities, with Aalborg being the only one to show a spatial concentration of youth unemployment within its territory.

As part of the statistical agenda to measure well-being in cities, this study builds on the OECD framework of How's Life In Your Region? and subsequently adapts such a framework to the scale of functional urban areas. The measurement of well-being distribution at city level as presented in this chapter brings about several challenges, especially when the aim is to provide statistics that can be compared across different administrative units. Statistical information provided at a very small and regular scale is crucial to measure well-being within cities. In this respect, grid-level data constitutes a benchmark scale at which to provide statistical information, since it is adaptable to work at different geographies. Increasing the provision of this type of data by national statistical offices would certainly help in understanding the relevance of local conditions on individuals' quality of life.

Note

1. Data provided by the Region of Southern Denmark.

References

Andersen, H.T., L. Winther (2010), "Crisis in the Resurgent City? The Rise of Copenhagen", *International Journal of Urban and Regional Research*, Vol. 34, No.3, pp. 693-700.

Chetty, R., N. Hendren and L.F. Katz (2015), "The effects of exposure to better neighborhoods on children: New evidence from the Moving to Opportunity Experiment", *NBER Working Papers*, No. 21 156, www.nber.org/papers/w21156.

de Vuijst, E., M. van Ham and R. Kleinhans (2015), "The moderating effect of higher education on intergenerational spatial inequality", *IZA Discussion Papers*, No. 9 557, http://ftp.iza.org/dp9557.pdf.

Faggian, A., M.R. Olfert and M. Partridge (2012), "Inferring regional well-being from individual revealed preferences: The 'voting with your feet' approach", *Cambridge Journal of Regions, Economy and Society*, Vol. 5/1, pp. 163-180, http://dx.doi.org/10.1093/cjres/rsr016.

Glaeser, E.L. and J. Vigdor (2012), "The end of the segregated century: Racial separation in America's neighborhoods, 1890-2010", *Civic Report*, No. 66, Center for State and Local Leadership at the Manhattan Institute, New York, www.manhattan-institute.org/pdf/cr_66.pdf.

Hansen, H.K., and L. Winther (2010), "The Spaces of Urban Economic Geographies: Industrial Transformation in the Outer City of Copenhagen", *Danish Journal of Geography*, 107(2), 45-48.

Kain, J. (1968), "Housing segregation, Negro employment, and metropolitan decentralization." *Quarterly Journal of Economics* Vol. 82, pp. 175-197.

Logan, J.R. and B.J. Stults (2011), *The Persistence of Segregation in the Metropolis: New Findings from the 2010 Census*, Russell Sage Foundation, New York.

Massey, D.S., J. Rothwell and T. Domina (2009), "The changing bases of segregation in the United States", *Annals of the American Academy of Political and Social Science*, Vol. 626/1, pp. 74-90, http://dx.doi.org/10.1177/0002716209343558.

McKenzie, E. (2016), "The relationships between the rise of private communities and increasing socioeconomic stratification", in: McCarthy, G.W., G.K. Ingram and S.A. Moody (eds.), *Land and the City*, Proceedings of the 2014 Land Policy Conference, Lincoln Institute.

Morrison, P.S. (2015), "The inequality debate. The neglected role of residential sorting", *Policy Quarterly*, Vol. 11/2, pp. 72-79, http://igps.victoria.ac.nz/publications/files/05ff5e0d1bb.pdf.

OECD (2016), *Making Cities Work for All: Data and Actions for Inclusive Growth*, OECD Publishing, Paris, http://dx.doi.org/10.1787/9789264263260-en.

Paul, K.I and K. Moser (2009), "Unemployment impairs mental health: Meta-analyses", *Journal of Vocational Behavior*, Vol. 74/3, pp. 264-282, http://dx.doi.org/10.1016/j.jvb.2009.01.001.

Rothwell, J.T. and D.J. Massey (2010), "Density zoning and class segregation in U.S. metropolitan areas", *Social Science Quarterly*, Vol. 91/5, pp. 1 123-1 143, http://dx.doi.org/10.1111/j.1540-6237.2010.00724.x.

Sharkey, P. (2008), "The intergenerational transmission of context", *American Journal of Sociology*, Vol. 113/4, pp. 931-969, http://inequality.stanford.edu/_media/pdf/Reference%20Media/Sharkey_2008.pdf.

Tammaru, T. et al. (eds.) (2016), *Socio-Economic Segregation in European Capital Cities: East Meets West*, Routledge, New York.

Tiebout, C. (1956), "A pure theory of local expenditures", *Journal of Public Economy*, Vol. 64/5, pp. 416-424, http://dx.doi.org/10.1086/257839.

van Ham, M. et al. (eds.) (2012), *Neighbourhood Effects Research: New Perspectives*, Springer, Dordrecht.

Vartanian, T.P., P.W. Buck and P. Gleason (2007), "Intergenerational neighborhood-type mobility: Examining differences between blacks and whites", *Housing Studies*, Vol. 22, pp. 833-856, http://dx.doi.org/10.1080/02673030701474792.

Veneri, P. (2015), "Urban spatial structure in OECD cities: Is urban population decentralising or clustering?", *OECD Regional Development Working Papers*, No. 2015/01, OECD Publishing, Paris, http://dx.doi.org/10.1787/5js3d834r3q7-en.

Winther, L. (2007), "Location Dynamics of Business Services in the Urban Landscape of Copenhagen: Imaginary Spaces of Location", *BELGEO*, Vol. 1, pp. 51-72.

Chapter 4.

Towards a wider use of well-being metrics for cities and regions: Challenges and way forward

This chapter provides a short summary on the challenges and way forward in using well-being measures in policy making at the local or city scale. It also present some examples of initiatives carried out in Danish regions and municipalities where a well-being framework was adopted.

Policy making is about making people's lives better. When taking decisions about schools, infrastructure or health services, concrete knowledge of what citizens think, appreciate or are missing can help identify the problems, the strengths and the challenges faced by a community. Well-being indicators can help foster this knowledge and understand the differences between living conditions in the large and small towns, in the city-regions and in the more remote areas. Statistical information at the local level can be used for several purposes and by different levels of government. Among these purposes is the identification of objectives of policy, the translation of such objectives into measurable indicators, the monitoring of how a given policy is effective based on outcomes and the empowerment of communities, which ultimately can help build trust in public institutions.

When referred to the local scale, the use of well-being indicators can also enhance the dialogue between citizens and policy makers on how a city, town or other types of places can be managed to strengthen people's well-being. Different areas have different issues to deal with as urbanisation challenges municipalities differently. The different areas within Danish city-regions are generally attracting population and increasing demand for public services, as they are places where jobs are concentrating the most and where people are moving from more remote areas. Other more peripheral municipalities are challenged by increasing pressures to provide public services in conditions of stagnating or declining population and productivity. In this context, measuring well-being implies trying to understand people's experiences and expectations in the different places, which are important for policy makers when they take decisions that directly affect people's lives today while creating the conditions for growth and development in the future.

Recent examples on the use of a well-being approach in subnational policy making

In Denmark, well-being metrics have already been largely used in policy making. There are different phases or steps in the policy making process with which it is possible to identify a well-being measurement cycle. These phases include the translation of well-being objectives into policy-relevant indicators, the selection of indicators, the identification of targets or expected results, the monitoring of the progress and the engagement of citizens and communication of the results. The following paragraphs report only a few examples in a rich set of initiatives where a well-being approach is used by policy makers at different levels of government.

The Region of Southern Denmark has developed a comprehensive set of well-being indicators on the individual and territorial factors that enhance a "Good Life" of people. In support of Southern Denmark's multi-year Regional Growth and Development Strategy, the region assesses the opportunities of living a "Good Life" by measuring a wide variety of material conditions and quality of life through 15 socio-economic indicators and 25 perception-based indicators drawn from survey data. The regional statistical yearbook, Kontur, integrates well-being indicators that provide a detailed profile for each of the 22 municipalities of the region. The region, in partnership with Statistics Denmark and based on 20 000 interviews (around 1 000 per municipality), tries to understand what facilitates the life of its inhabitants. The main objective is that of creating good circumstances for the "Good Life" and to focus on the aspects that are more relevant for people and where results can be achieved through policy. The identification of the indicators is not the only step made by the region, which is already working to foster citizen engagement and to translate such indicators into concrete policy actions.

The Danish National Health Profile (*Hvordan har du det?*/How are you?) is a survey resulting from a collaboration between all Danish regions and is used to analyse the health status among their citizens and to develop policy plans. The survey provides statistical information which can be used also at the municipal level. For instance, the Central Denmark Region carries out analyses and prepares reports that give a picture of one or more municipalities regarding the perceived well-being of their citizens and especially their health status. The use of such data helps identify places where an intervention in the health sector is most needed and understand how the districts of care should be made for elderly people. The region will take this knowledge into account in designing its next health plan.

The adoption of a well-being approach in policy making is also observed at municipal level. Many examples can be found in Denmark. One of those is the municipality of Aarhus, which has identified two objectives that it is going to monitor over time: "Aarhus is a good city for all" and "in Aarhus, we have a high degree of citizenship". The next step would be that of identifying indicators and monitor results. The monitoring of the two objectives, which involves several stakeholders, including committees of citizens, should also help identify areas where the achievement is high or low. These targets will serve as guideposts for the development strategy of Aarhus, which aims at ensuring coherence between the history of the city, its values and the visions for the future.

Other examples can highlight that, even at local level, well-being initiatives could take advantage from a more intense use of measures. The Vision Strategy 2020 and the Growth Strategy 2020 are the two main topics undertaken by the municipality of Esbjerg. Strengthened by its World Energy Cities Partnership, which is a collaboration between 19 globally recognised "energy cities" around the world, the municipality of Esbjerg wants to invest in electric cars. On the other hand, efforts are being made to increase bus service, with the aim of avoiding that people, even when they have a job, feel isolated when back home. Esbjerg is also trying to provide help with social activities. For this purpose, a digital application has been created, the Esbjerg Live application, which is a guide to recreation and leisure across Esbjerg municipality with an overview of the associations, events and places, including those in the municipalities of Fanø and Varde.

Challenges and way forward

An important challenge that emerges when measuring people's quality of life is that the choice of indicators is very important and determines the extent to which such measurement matches people's own perceptions. For instance, there can be a significant difference between the level of income and the feeling of financial comfort and this difference can be particularly strong in rural areas, where living costs are lower. This discrepancy echoes the idea of "perhaps not very rich but very happy" and is linked with the relationship between subjective well-being (e.g. life satisfaction) and other more objective indicators of quality of life and material conditions (e.g. income, health, education, etc.). When assessing well-being through a dashboard of indicators, one main challenge is choosing the right target and the right indicator, with the objective that an improvement in one such indicator is also reflected in an improvement of subjective well-being. This requires better understanding the link between what can be measured and people's actual feelings in order to design an effective course of action. In this respect, it seems important to combine the individual and subjective point of views with the assessment of the conditions of a community. As citizens are part of a society, the conditions of the whole society in a city or in another local environment should not be left aside.

Another challenge is related to the scale at which to measure people's well-being in order to include both individual outcomes and place-based characteristics. In this respect, city-regions represent a relevant geography, though there are different views of city-regions, in particular on how they are constructed. For example, the city-region of Odense excludes some of the municipalities in Funen, which in some respects, especially those connected to regional identity and physical geography, could be considered part of the same system. Indeed, the boundaries of functional urban areas should be flexible and no perfect geography exists for all purposes. The identification of the Danish city-regions can serve as an experiment in this respect and provides a benchmark for a relevant geography for policy making, since such city-regions reflect where people live and work. What is more important is the fact that it is not the administrative boundaries of municipalities that control where one moves oneself around in Denmark. Municipalities can be even more effective if they work together to improve the well-being of their citizens. In this respect, the co-operation among municipalities in the different city-regions could be enhanced by the evidence that there are win-win relationships between the city cores and the surrounding commuting zones. The use of well-being indicators at small geographical level (e.g. municipalities) is a possible way to show how and in what domains such virtuous relationships can occur.

The way forward in the measurement of well-being at local level is that of bringing the new knowledge into play to further improve people's lives. A detailed knowledge of urban residents, business, service availability and other aspects provide the necessary solid basis for taking decisions to promote development in all places. It is therefore important to expand even more the evidence at the local level, up to the scale of municipalities. Such a knowledge base can be used by citizens, businesses, associations and other types of stakeholders playing an active role in a society. In the case of Danish city-regions, the measurement of well-being can help create a common identity in the city, aligned around a few but powerful common objectives, and strengthen co-operation and community among citizens.

In the provision and use of well-being indicators for policy making, both regional and local government have a role to play. Municipalities can benefit from the knowledge of the needs of their citizens, but often they do not have the resources to produce or elaborate such data. Regions are instead in a position of offering a common framework and tools to help them identify priorities and to foster a strong institutional dialogue.

Annex A.
Well-being snapshots of Danish cities

This annex presents a snapshot of well-being for each of the five Danish cities.

The dimensional indicators are normalised using the minimum and maximum values of each indicator for the latest year available and for all the Danish city-regions, and rescaled to a range from 85 to 115 according to two "goalposts" that represent the minimum and maximum values for all normalised indicators. In this way, by setting the observed national current value to 100, all the values in the Danish city-regions will lie in the interval [85;115] and values above (below) 100 will represent performance above (below) the national current average. The formula for the normalisation is the following.

Think of a well-being dimension composed of one indicator, the value of the indicator for the Danish city-region i in the latest year available can be represented by x_i. Since there are five city-regions, $i \in [1,2, \dots 5]$. If higher values of x_i represent higher well-being in terms of the indicator (e.g. life expectancy), the normalised value of x_i, denoted as z_i, can be obtained through the following formula:

$$z_i = 30 * \frac{x_i - min_i}{max_i - min_i} + 85$$

On the other hand, if higher values of x_i denote lower well-being as measured by the indicator (e.g. obesity rate), the normalised value of x_i is computed as the complement of the previous equation with respect to 200 (i.e. $z_i = 200 - 30 * \frac{x_i - min_i}{max_i - min_i} - 85$). Where min_i and max_i are respectively the minimum and maximum values of the indicator across city-regions (i.e. $\forall\, i \in [1,2, \dots 5]$). Then, one simply has to adjust this value in a way that the country normalised score in the latest year is equal to 100.

$$\bar{z}_i = z_i - (z_{i2} - 100)$$

where z_{i2} is the normalised (still not set to 100) value of the indicator for the country.

Aalborg

Well-being in Aalborg exceeds the national average in four dimensions and lags behind in five. Jobs outcomes are relatively low in Aalborg which has the highest unemployment rate among the Danish city-regions. A homicide rate equal to twice the national value explains the poor performance in the safety dimension. The city-region of Aalborg also ranks among the last in the dimensions of civic engagement and income. However, the lowest level of air pollution and the highest number of rooms per person drive the great performances in environment and housing respectively.

Figure A.1. **Well-being in Aalborg, 2015 or latest available year**

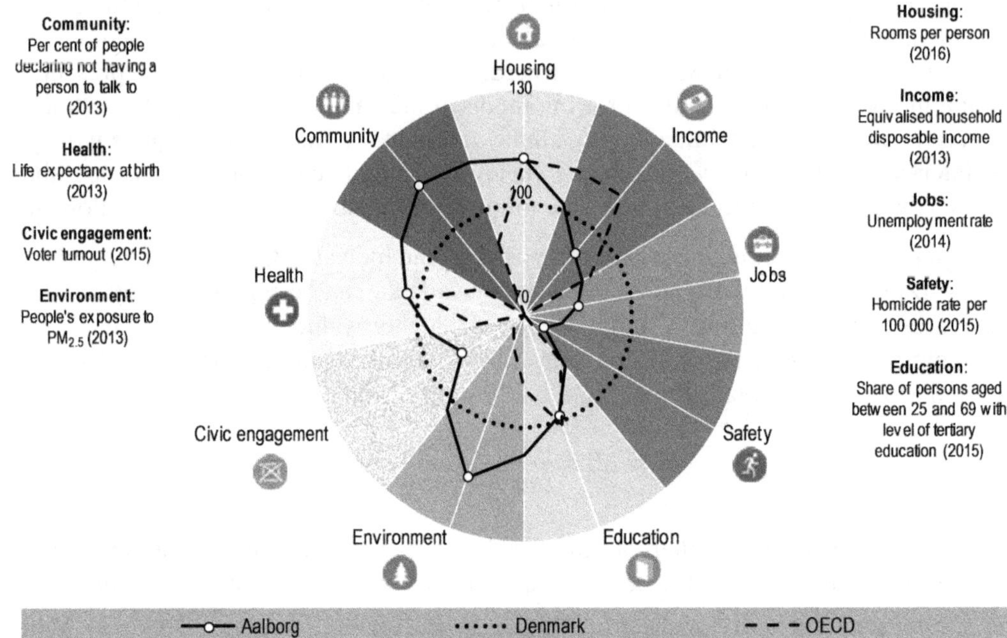

Notes: The score by dimension is computed by normalising the chosen indicator illustrating the well-being dimension. The national average value in each dimension is set to 100 (black dashed line); the city-regions' values vary between 85 and 115. A higher score indicates better performance in a dimension relative to all the other cities. For reasons of data availability, only nine dimensions are represented here.

Aalborg has the second lowest level of spatial segregation by income among Danish city-regions, meaning that the income distribution across neighbourhoods is one of the most even. However, the city-region of Aalborg performs in line with the average of the other cities in terms of spatial segregation by employment status. Neither the core nor the commuting zone has a more deep-seated unemployed vs. employed Dissimilarity Index. Nonetheless, high concentrations of youth unemployment are observed within the commuting zone of Aalborg and this is the only case for a Danish city-region.

Table A.1. **Segregation indexes within Aalborg**

Lower rank means lower segregation

Measure	City-region	Core	Commuting zone
Position in spatial segregation by income (out of 5)	4		
Position in unemployed vs. employed dissimilarity (out of 5)	3	3	3
Number of concentrated areas of youth unemployment	3	0	3

Aarhus

Well-being in Aarhus exceeds the national performance in seven of the nine dimensions, while it lags slightly behind in housing and safety. The strong performance in health, education and civic engagement (first ranked city-region) is driven by the highest life expectancy at birth among the Danish city-regions, 42% of Aarhus' residents aged 25-69 with a level of tertiary education, and more than 86% of voter turnout.

Figure A.2. **Well-being in Aarhus, 2015 or latest available year**

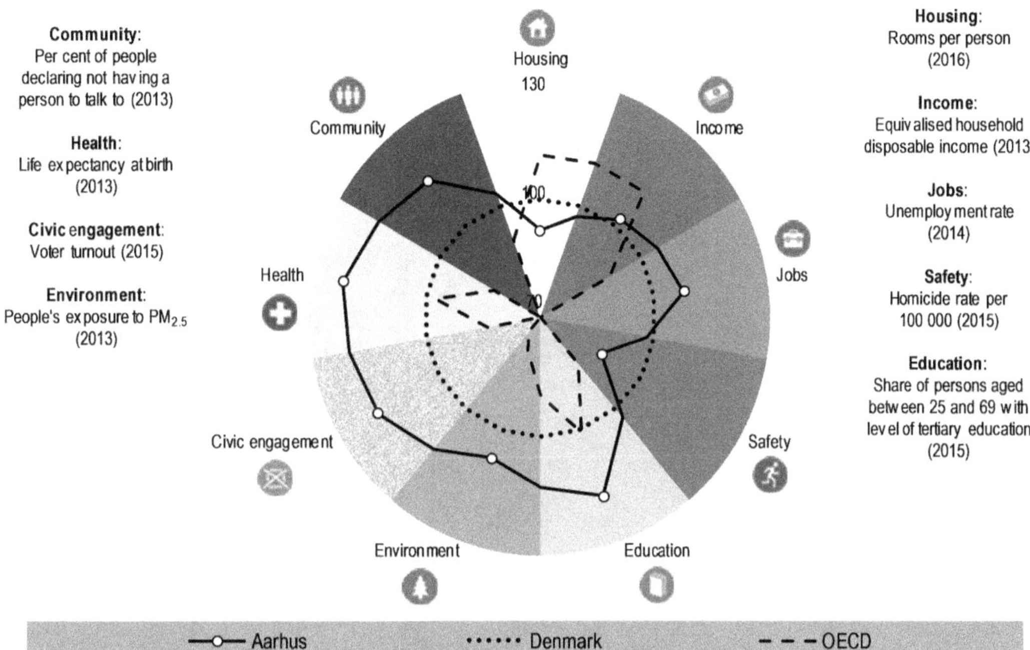

Notes: The score by dimension is computed by normalising the chosen indicator illustrating the well-being dimension. The national average value in each dimension is set to 100 (black dashed line); the city-regions' values vary between 85 and 115. A higher score indicates better performance in a dimension relative to all the other cities. For reasons of data availability, only nine dimensions are represented here.

Aarhus has the highest level of spatial segregation by income compared to the other Danish city-regions. However, the city-region of Aarhus has the second lowest level of spatial segregation in terms of employment status. More specifically, the core and the commuting zone of Aarhus have the second lowest unemployed vs. employed Dissimilarity Indexes in their respective ranks. High concentrations of youth unemployment are not observed within the entire city-region.

Table A.2. **Segregation indexes within Aarhus**

Lower rank means lower segregation

Measure	City-region	Core	Commuting zone
Position in spatial segregation by income (out of 5)	5		
Position in unemployed vs. employed dissimilarity (out of 5)	2	2	2
Number of concentrated areas of youth unemployment	0	0	0

Copenhagen

In five of the nine available well-being dimensions, Copenhagen performs better than or similar to the national average. By contrast, its performance is lagging in the housing, environment and health dimensions. Copenhagen ranks last among the five city-regions in environment, as the level of air pollution is the highest. The strong performance in income and community (first ranked city-region) is driven by the highest value of household disposable income and the lowest share of residents declaring not having a person to talk to, respectively.

Figure A.3. **Well-being in Copenhagen, 2015 or latest available year**

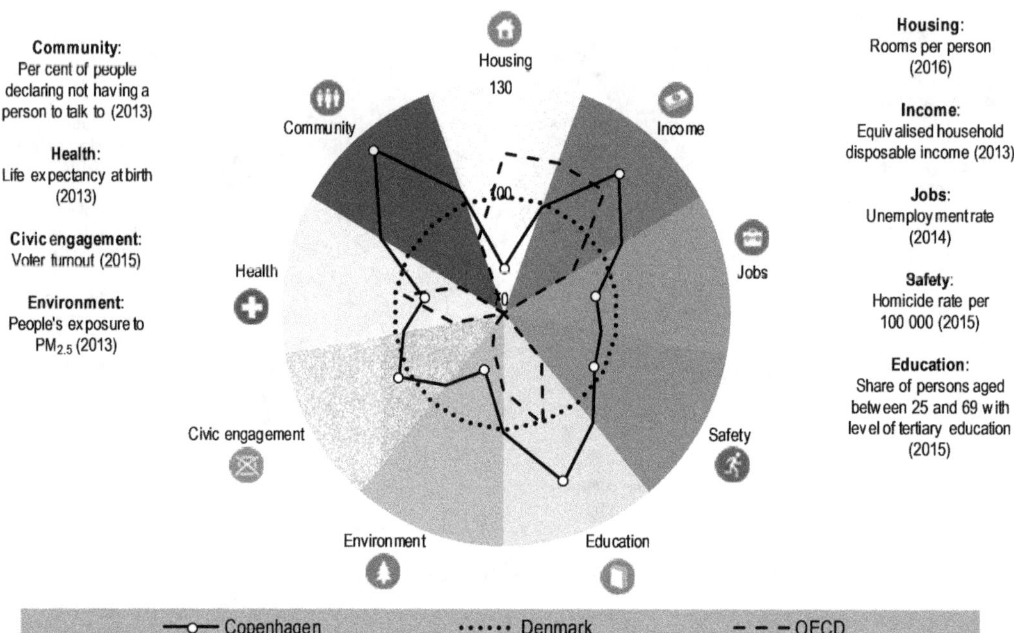

Notes: The score by dimension is computed by normalising the chosen indicator illustrating the well-being dimension. The national average value in each dimension is set to 100 (black dashed line); the city-regions' values vary between 85 and 115. A higher score indicates better performance in a dimension relative to all the other cities. For reasons of data availability, only nine dimensions are represented here.

In terms of income segregation, Copenhagen ranks third compared to the other Danish city-regions. However, the city-region of Copenhagen has the second highest level of spatial segregation in terms of employment status, which is particularly high in the commuting zone with respect to the city core. More specifically, the commuting zone of the city-region has the highest unemployed vs. employed Dissimilarity Index whereas its core has the lowest. However, high concentrations of youth unemployment are not observed within Copenhagen (no hotspots in the entire city region).

Table A.3. **Segregation indexes within Copenhagen**

Lower rank means lower segregation

Measure	City-region	Core	Commuting zone
Position in spatial segregation by income (out of 5)	3		
Position in unemployed vs. employed dissimilarity (out of 5)	4	1	5
Number of concentrated areas of youth unemployment	0	0	0

Esbjerg

With respect to the national average, well-being in Esbjerg is higher in three dimensions: jobs, safety and environment. It displays national average performance in income, health and community, and lags behind in the remaining three dimensions. The good jobs outcomes (ranked first out of five) are driven by the lowest unemployment rate among the Danish city-regions. In contrast, Esbjerg has the lowest share of residents aged 25-69 with a tertiary educational attainment.

Figure A.4. **Well-being in Esbjerg, 2015 or latest available year**

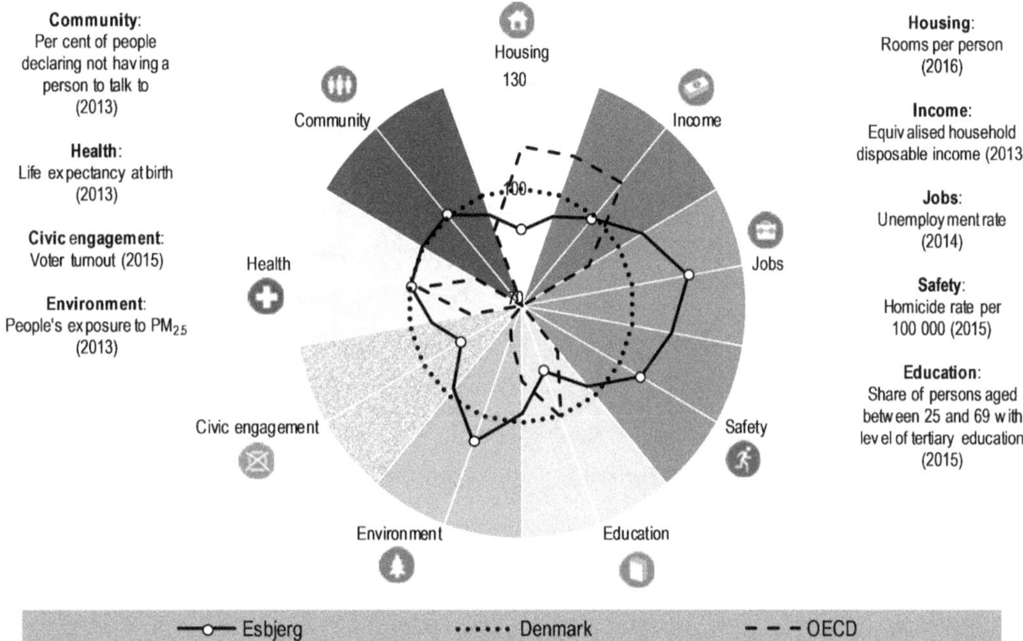

Notes: The score by dimension is computed by normalising the chosen indicator illustrating the well-being dimension. The national average value in each dimension is set to 100 (black dashed line); the city-regions' values vary between 85 and 115. A higher score indicates better performance in a dimension relative to all the other cities. For reasons of data availability, only nine dimensions are represented here.

Esbjerg has the lowest level of spatial segregation by income among Danish city-regions. On the contrary, the city-region of Esbjerg has the highest level of spatial segregation in terms of employment status. More specifically, the core of Esbjerg has the highest unemployed vs. employed Dissimilarity Index and the commuting zone the second highest. However, clusters of high concentrations of youth unemployment are not observed within the entire city-region.

Table A.4. **Segregation indexes within Esbjerg**

Lower rank means lower segregation

Measure	City-region	Core	Commuting zone
Position in spatial segregation by income (out of 5)	1		
Position in unemployed vs. employed dissimilarity (out of 5)	5	5	4
Number of concentrated areas of youth unemployment	0	0	0

Odense

Well-being in the city-region of Odense exceeds the national average only in the housing dimension, while it performs similarly in almost all the remaining dimensions, except for income and jobs where it lags significantly behind. The city-region ranks second in housing outcomes among the Danish city-regions, due to a relatively high number of rooms per person. On the other hand, Odense ranks last in income as it shows the lowest performance in terms of household disposable income. Residents also report the lowest value of community (social relations) among Danish cities.

Figure A.5. **Well-being in Odense, 2015 or latest available year**

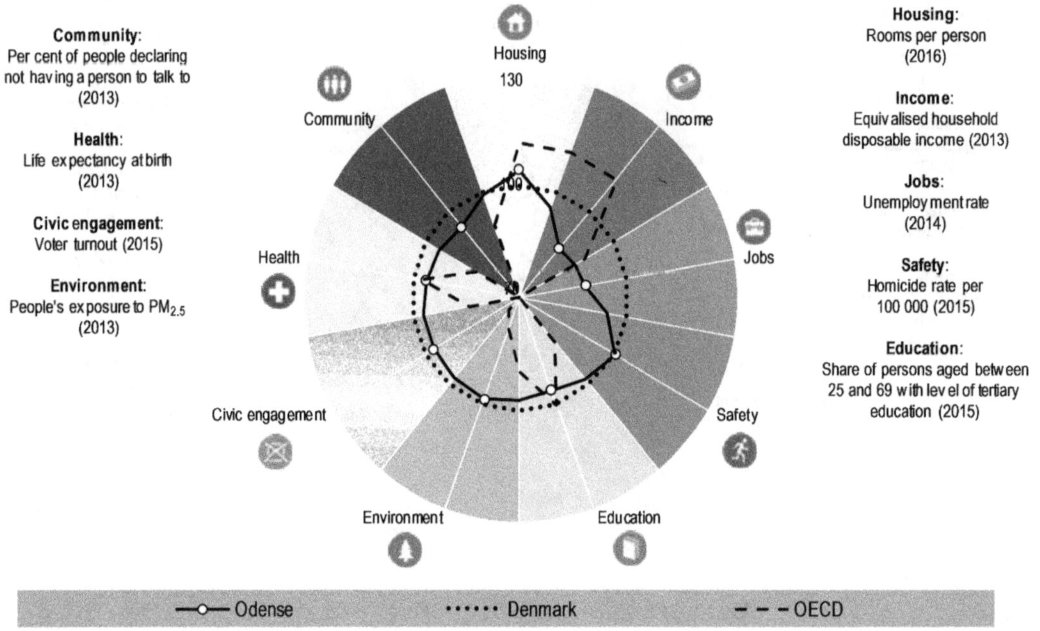

Community: Per cent of people declaring not having a person to talk to (2013)

Health: Life expectancy at birth (2013)

Civic engagement: Voter turnout (2015)

Environment: People's exposure to $PM_{2.5}$ (2013)

Housing: Rooms per person (2016)

Income: Equivalised household disposable income (2013)

Jobs: Unemployment rate (2014)

Safety: Homicide rate per 100 000 (2015)

Education: Share of persons aged between 25 and 69 with level of tertiary education (2015)

Housing 130 | Income | Jobs | Safety | Education | Environment | Civic engagement | Health | Community

—o— Odense ······ Denmark – – – OECD

Notes: The score by dimension is computed by normalising the chosen indicator illustrating the well-being dimension. The national average value in each dimension is set to 100 (black dashed line); the city-regions' values vary between 85 and 115. A higher score indicates better performance in a dimension relative to all the other cities. For reasons of data availability, only nine dimensions are represented here.

In terms of spatial segregation by income, Odense has the second lowest level compared to the other Danish city-regions. In addition, the city-region of Odense has the lowest level of spatial segregation in terms of employment status, which is, however, particularly high in the core with respect to the commuting zone. More specifically, the commuting zone of Odense has the lowest unemployed vs. employed Dissimilarity Index, whereas its core has the second highest. High concentrations of youth unemployment are not observed within the entire city-region.

Table A.5. **Segregation indexes within Odense**

Lower rank means lower segregation

Measure	City-region	Core	Commuting zone
Position in spatial segregation by income (out of 5)	2		
Position in unemployed vs. employed dissimilarity (out of 5)	1	4	1
Number of concentrated areas of youth unemployment	0	0	0

A summary snapshot of well-being in Danish cities

The city-region of Aarhus ranks first among the Danish city-regions in education, civic engagement and health, and never last in any well-being dimension. The city-region of Copenhagen ranks last among the Danish city-regions in housing, environment and health, but first in income and community.

Figure A.6. **Performance of Danish cities by well-being dimension**

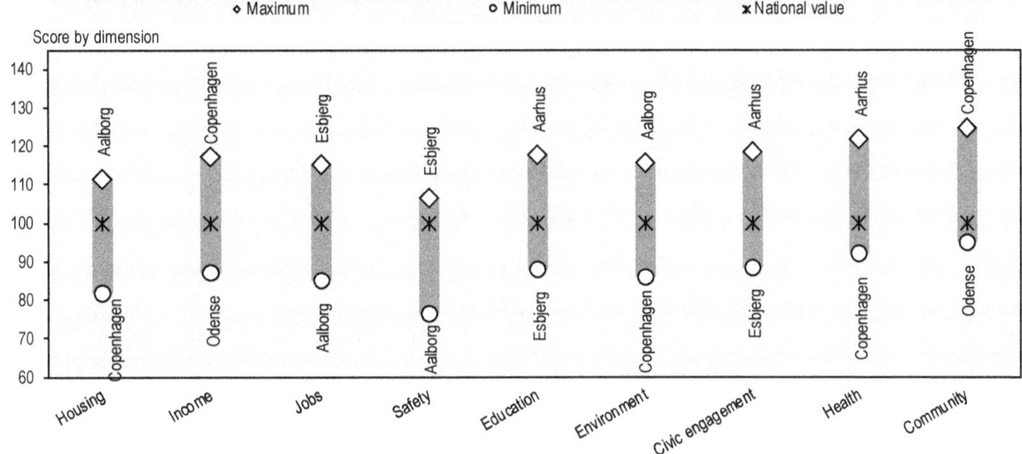

Note: The score by dimension is computed by normalising the chosen indicator illustrating the well-being dimension. The country's value in each dimension is set to 100.

Source: See Table 2.A1.1: Summary of data sources and scales.

The high-performing Danish cities fare better than the OECD average in all eight well-being dimensions. The low-performing Danish cities also fare better than the OECD average in four well-being dimensions, with the exception of health, education, housing and income.

Table A.6. **How do the top and bottom cities in Denmark fare on the well-being indicators?**

	Danish city-regions		Country average	OECD average
	Top	Bottom		
Environment				
Level of air pollution in $PM_{2.5}$ (µg/m³), 2013	5.9	12.5	9.4	14.1
Safety				
Homicide rate (per 100 000 people), 2015	0.6	1.6	0.8	4.1
Community				
Persons declaring not having a person to talk to (%), 2013	0.04	0.05	0.05	
Health				
Life expectancy at birth (years), 2013	81.0	79.8	80.1	80.0
Education				
Persons aged 25-64 with at least a tertiary education (%), 2015	0.42	0.27	0.33	0.34
Jobs				
Unemployment rate (%), 2014	0.03	0.05	0.04	0.07
Housing				
Rooms per person, 2016	1.8	1.3	1.6	1.8
Income				
Equivalised household disposable income (in USD PPP), 2013	26 848	23 158	24 750	26 138
Civic engagement				
Voters in last national election (%), 2015	0.86	0.84	0.85	0.68

ORGANISATION FOR ECONOMIC CO-OPERATION AND DEVELOPMENT

The OECD is a unique forum where governments work together to address the economic, social and environmental challenges of globalisation. The OECD is also at the forefront of efforts to understand and to help governments respond to new developments and concerns, such as corporate governance, the information economy and the challenges of an ageing population. The Organisation provides a setting where governments can compare policy experiences, seek answers to common problems, identify good practice and work to co-ordinate domestic and international policies.

The OECD member countries are: Australia, Austria, Belgium, Canada, Chile, the Czech Republic, Denmark, Estonia, Finland, France, Germany, Greece, Hungary, Iceland, Ireland, Israel, Italy, Japan, Korea, Latvia, Luxembourg, Mexico, the Netherlands, New Zealand, Norway, Poland, Portugal, the Slovak Republic, Slovenia, Spain, Sweden, Switzerland, Turkey, the United Kingdom and the United States. The European Union takes part in the work of the OECD.

OECD Publishing disseminates widely the results of the Organisation's statistics gathering and research on economic, social and environmental issues, as well as the conventions, guidelines and standards agreed by its members.

OECD PUBLISHING, 2, rue André-Pascal, 75775 PARIS CEDEX 16
(04 2016 10 1 P) ISBN 978-92-64-26523-3 – 2016

www.ingramcontent.com/pod-product-compliance
Lightning Source LLC
LaVergne TN
LVHW081419110826
845149LV00010B/1803